A History of Horses
Told by Horses

Horse Sense for Humans

H. A. Levin

Illustrations by Daniella K. Thireou

Morgan James Publishing • NEW YORK

ALSO BY H. A. LEVIN

Quotations for Successful Living

How to Live Life

Letters to an Angel

How to Love Life

A HISTORY OF HORSES
TOLD BY HORSES

Library of Congress Control Number: 20089336430
ISBN: 978-1-60037-475-3 (Paperback)
ISBN: 978-1-60037-477-7 (Hardcover)
ISBN: 978-1-60037-476-0 (Audio)

Published by:

MORGAN · JAMES
THE ENTREPRENEURIAL PUBLISHER™
www.morganjamespublishing.com

Morgan James Publishing, LLC
1225 Franklin Ave Suite 325
Garden City, NY 11530-1693
Toll Free 800-485-4943
www.MorganJamesPublishing.com

Cover Design by:
Sue Krauer

Cover Photo by:
Glenn Asakawa/ *The Denver Post*

Interior Design by:
Rachel Lopez
rachel@r2cdesign.com

In an effort to support local communities, raise awareness and funds, Morgan James Publishing donates one percent of all book sales for the life of each book to Habitat for Humanity.

Get involved today, visit www.HelpHabitatForHumanity.org.

A Note to the Readers

As you will see as you read on through this book, horses are steadfast in their devotion to humanity, with a very special affinity for women. They wish to share their feelings and hopes for the future of mankind in relation to the earth and its many species.

Many people have reservations or are skeptical about interspecies communication. But, in fact, anyone can learn to communicate with animals. This special awareness is easier to learn than you may think. Understanding and communications can be accomplished through acceptance, patience, trust, genuine caring, an open mind and centering yourself 'in the moment.' This type of communication is within your grasp if you are willing to open your heart.

In many places throughout the world, the horseshoe is placed above doorways as a symbol of luck. Throughout the United States, England, Ireland, and a few other places, the horseshoe is placed facing up, or the luck will run out. In much of the rest of the world, the horseshoe is placed facing down, so the luck can pour over you. Thus, we have alternately placed the horseshoe graphic up and down to satisfy the luck for all the peoples of the world.

Always respect the rights of horses and landowners. Ask permission to access private property, and seek a caregiver's permission before approaching their horse.

The information in this manuscript is as accurate as possible. The author and publisher accept no responsibility for any loss, injury, or inconvenience by anyone reading this book.

Dedicated to
Animal Lovers

TABLE OF CONTENTS

"The soul is the same in all living creatures,
although the body of each is different."

- HIPPOCRATES

Meeting Bess

Steamboat Lake, Colorado

A t dawn, after a night camping in a high Rocky Mountain meadow, I awoke to a myriad of wildflowers and a mist rising from Steamboat Lake. I hopped a fence into a pasture to enjoy a stunning sunrise. Suddenly, I felt a presence behind me and turned to defend myself, but was relieved to discover that I had been spooked by a grazing mare. Feeling foolish to be frightened by a horse, I turned back to face the rising sun. The mare circled me while slowly tugging some grass. This was a large field; apparently I was in a lush spot. Not wanting to block her way, I stepped aside. The mare again moved closer and pawed the ground.

When I focused on the horse, she stepped back so that I could admire her. Over sixteen hands high, easily a thousand pounds, she had a healthy build, a shiny red roan coat with matching mane and tail, and a narrow white blaze on her face—a really lovely horse. When our eyes met, a connection was made far beyond that of

1

hearing or seeing. Her enormous eye held me transfixed for a long, surreal moment. Then she greeted me with a knowing look, a breath of warm air on my face, and words that filled my head, "Hello. Welcome to my field."

Looking around and seeing no one, I responded mentally, "Thank you."

Silently, she continued, "I love this pasture. Did you enjoy the sunrise?"

"Yes. I especially like watching the mist slowly dissipate to reveal Hahn's Peak—that mountain that looks like an upside down snow cone. It was gorgeous," I said as though chatting with an old friend.

My fingers tingled: I was communicating without speaking aloud, and connecting in a way I had never experienced before, yet it felt natural to speak silently. Could this be telepathy—with a horse?

"Sunrises here are beautiful all year long. You should see the fields after a night of snowfall when everything looks gift-wrapped in white."

"I know it well," I smiled, and then looked around to see whether anyone was watching our encounter. I felt embarrassed about talking with a horse.

"Don't worry about your friends. They can't tell that we're conversing. Lots of people come here for parties and weddings, but I've never seen you."

"I have been traveling for several years," I answered while edging away.

The mare nudged my shoulder, stomped the ground, and stated, "You're in my pasture now, and it would be polite if you paid a little attention to me!"

Not knowing how to respond, I extended my hand and said, "Hi, I'm Hal."

She swung her head to nestle her nose into the palm of my out-stretched hand. Patiently, I waited while she breathed on and sniffed my fingers. The whiskers on the end of her nose tickled; her velvety lips felt like exploring fingers. After a few moments, she slipped the supple part of her jaw into my hand, and with a shake of her head, said hello.

I didn't move as she continued, "People call me Bess. It certainly took you a while to notice me, but then, some people never pay attention, and very few listen to horses' thoughts."

"I didn't know horses had thoughts."

"We have many—and feelings, too."

"What do you think about?"

"Many people claim they want to listen, but really their attention is very short-lived, because they only want to take control or go for a ride. Do you really want to know?"

"Yes, please tell me."

"Some of the things we think about are love, food, freedom, and our hopes for the future. May I ask what you do for a living?"

"My passion is writing books that inspire people."

"I like that. Hal, there's a spot I can't reach that's bothering me. Can you help?" Bess swung her head toward a stiff knot of caked mud and hair high on her neck. I broke the mud loose and stroked her hair smooth.

"Thanks for the help. People are lucky to have hands and fingers to do all kinds of things we horses can't. But as partners, we can accomplish so much together. What I mean is, there are times when one plus one is more than two. Do you understand?"

"Please explain it to me," I answered while shaking my analytical head.

"I like it when you use body movements to talk. Horses converse a great deal with body language. In the wild, it's safer to speak visually than aloud and reveal our position to predators.

"When I say one plus one is more than two, I mean two beings, like horses, humans, or a horse and a human, working together can accomplish much more than each individually. Do you understand?"

"Yes, I do," I answered, laughing at myself for being tutored by a horse.

"Hal, equines have been searching for a person to write a book about the history of horses, told by horses," she stated and purposely pushed me so I had to stagger to regain my balance. A low nicker of laughter escaped her. "Are you interested?"

Totally intrigued, but with no idea what I was getting myself into, I ineffectually returned her nudge and answered, "Sure, but I didn't know horses knew about books."

"Our far-reaching knowledge may surprise you. Horses are one of the most important animals in human history. If you write our story, we will tell you why it's imperative that our message be shared."

"Horses have a plan?"

"Yes, we are on a mission to empower women."

"Why?"

"In order to save humanity and the world, for there is too much abuse by humans. Your complex societies have exploited women, children, and animals for too long. Horses have witnessed man's growing disregard for the interconnectedness of all beings, and the gross imbalance this has created in the natural world. Humanity now negatively impacts the environment like no other species. The Earth needs more open-minded people who realize that all life on this planet is connected.

"One of our goals is to partner with, and to strengthen, compassionate women, who value cooperation, nurturing, and love, because we believe women can change humanity's course in a positive way. Empowered women demand equality and walk side by side with men. We want to help people live more in the moment, increase their ability to communicate, learn from each other, and be healed.

"Horses help humans gain self-confidence by accepting them no matter what they look like or how much money they have. An equine friend can help to increase a person's intuition and self-esteem. Women, in particular, need encouragement to fully develop their self-confidence. Horses also teach females how to use fear as a survival tool. We encourage women to form a family of female friends for their personal protection and spiritual growth. You can learn a lot from animals, if you have an open mind. All we want is peace, love, and the restoration of nature."

"Can all of that be achieved by riding a horse?"

"Our most important work takes place when people are on the ground. Riding, which borrows freedom from a horse, may strengthen the bond, but should be considered an earned honor. Equestrians are not riders without horses. The best things that a person can do before mounting are to show kindness, have patience, and try to see the world from our standpoint."

"But most people can't afford to own a horse."

"That's okay; establishing a friendly relationship is much more important than ownership."

"When did horses start helping people?"

"Long ago, when we were threatened with extinction by human hunters, horses chose domestication for survival. We slaved for men for many centuries while trying to nurture their compassionate spirit, but it is slow work. Do you realize how out of balance Earth is?"

"Yes, sometimes the world seems crazy."

"If the human race continues to spin out of control, people will cause the extinction of many more species, and ultimately, threaten humanity's existence. Will you help us save the world?"

"Certainly, but how?"

"Just follow our instructions and write. Don't ever give up, even if people make fun of you."

"But will horses help men, too?"

"We want to empower all people. But we connect with, and inspire, most of the females we meet, which is why so many women have extraordinary relationships with horses. It is up to courageous women, with the help of horses, to save the Earth by leading humanity towards a more peaceful, life sustaining path. Some men don't want to grant women equal rights for fear of losing their own power. Yet in reality, equality leads to respect and true unity among people."

"But why would you want a man to tell your story rather than a woman?"

"Women have written many inspirational stories about their empowering experiences with horses. But our message may be more credible in a book authored by a man. A male would have little to gain by relating the history of horses from the horses' perspective. In fact, much of our story reflects the dark side of man's history. Will you write for us?"

"Yes, but where do I start?"

"First, learn to live in the moment, which is when a person may hear our voice or feel our emotions. When you are ready, we will recount horse history to you from its earliest beginnings. We will describe how we evolved, how wild horses live, and why we decided to become an important part of human history. Our story will show that while we no longer need to be a beast of burden, horses are now more important than ever to people. We are good teachers, and our story will lead you to a new level of enlightenment."

As several horses crested a hill at the far end of the field, Bess said, "Now I need to spend time with my family. Please, will you return here tomorrow at dawn to continue?"

"Yes, I will."

"Thank you," Bess whinnied. She then made a perfect pirouette and galloped across the field.

"Far back, far back in our dark soul the horse prances…"

- D. H. Lawrence

DAWN

Bess; Steamboat Lake, Colorado

Early the following morning, I eagerly scaled the fence into the dew-soaked field. The growing light revealed the colorful countryside. Mountains cloaked in aspen and pine surrounded the horses' grassy pasture. Bess was grazing peacefully with her family. She bobbed her head in recognition and happily ambled over to join me.

"My friends and I want to share dawn with you, because it reminds us every day of Dawn, the mother of our species, who roamed North America. She was one of the first mammals to appear after the dinosaurs' demise, almost sixty million years ago. Hey, where are your writing implements?"

"I left them in my van," I answered, rolling my eyes.

"What kind of writer are you?" Bess asked, rolling her eyes in a funny mimicry of me.

On the way back to my van I felt peaceful, and remembered that I had brought carrots as a surprise. In my excitement, I had left them, too. When I emerged from my vehicle, a fox trotted across the road from the direction of the horses. She slowed, and then froze by the edge of the trees. Her bushy tail, extended straight out, almost doubled her small size, and mirrored her face in coloration. At a glance, it was hard to tell which way the fox faced. She surprised me when she looked in my direction and spoke.

"So you are the one!" She then disappeared into the woods without waiting for a reply.

Stupefied by the fox's comment, I looked up to see a great blue heron floating overhead. With his huge wing span and effortless flight, he circled high above. Was I imagining that this beautiful bird also spoke to me, encouraging me to listen to the horses, as he glided over the treetops?

Contemplating the fox's and the heron's words, I offered Bess a carrot.

"I hope you have enough for everyone," she said as she crunched the carrot. The other horses' ears perked and pointed toward us.

The tall lead stallion came forward. Before taking a carrot, he breathed in my essence and introduced himself as Cash. He had a cream-colored coat, a wide white blaze on his intelligent face, and a pink-tipped nose. Bess then introduced her two-year-old son, Sundance, who was a beautiful colt with a white crescent moon between his eyes.

Dainty came next, a small, very friendly chestnut mare, whose mane and tail matched her thick coat. With her came Baby, Dainty's very shy youngest. She explained that Baby's front left foot had accidentally been stepped on when she was a foal; hence she had a permanent limp. Baby haltingly reached for her carrot and quickly retreated behind her mother. Dainty's firstborn, Kai, was a classic bay with black mane and tail. He stood almost as tall as Cash. Dainty's other daughter, Star, was named for the small white spot on her forehead, and had the same coloring as Kai. Both were very pretty.

Boy, a beautiful but shy Appaloosa, was last. His eyes were filled with fear as he stretched his neck for the treat. Bess told me that Boy had been mistreated by his previous owner and still had misgivings about people.

"On my way to the car, I thought I heard a fox and a heron talk to me. I still don't know what to think of speaking silently," I said.

"Remember, life is especially rewarding when you live in the moment and appreciate that everything is connected. Now we want to tell you the ancient history of our species, beginning with Dawn, and later show you the ways in which horses have helped humans throughout history. We asked the fox to come by to demonstrate Dawn's small size.

"Dawn had a short neck and a dark striped coat of earth-toned browns. She had four soft-padded toes on her front feet and three soft-padded toes on her back feet, which made her surefooted and kept her from sinking in the boggy marshes and wetlands that covered much of her range.

"The climate was very different during Dawn's time: semi-tropical flora created thick rain forests of huge cypress and gigantic deciduous trees. The forests provided abundant, soft, leafy bushes—tender food just right for early equines' small browsing teeth.

"Except for new mothers and their young, prehistoric horses lived singly and depended heavily on camouflage for protection from predators. Concealment served our ancestors well for many generations. Yet early horses always feared what might be around the next tree. Since life could end at any moment, ancient equines slept standing up and only for a few minutes at a time. They lived an average of just three to four years.

"From the beginning, horses were a nonconfrontational species of herbivores, or vegetarians. We loved our fellow creatures and formed symbiotic relationships whenever possible. For example, we allow sparrows to perch on our backs to eat ticks and other biting parasites from our skin. Birds are good sentries, because they give early alarm calls when danger lurks.

"Over millions of years, as the Earth became drier, forests receded and were replaced by extensive grassy plains. With short legs and splayed feet, the equines could not outrun most predators and became easy prey in the open. Defenseless, Dawn and her family needed to adapt or perish.

"Dawn saved our species. She encouraged her family to change from browsers to grazers, since grasses had become abundant. Her family developed larger teeth and strong jaws to chew and break down food. Grazing meant that horses had to lower their heads to eat instead of stretching out and up to reach leaves, which put us at great risk. We could not watch for danger very well with our heads down. For safety, Dawn persuaded her family to graze together as a group, or band. As horses became more socialized, we learned to live in close proximity, so carnivores had more trouble approaching undetected. Also, an entire group of horses could defend the foals rather than each individual mother having the sole responsibility. Thus, equines became leaders among the developing grazers and were the first to form family and bachelor bands.

"In order to migrate safely to richer grazing grounds, several bands came together to form a herd. Herding increased interaction, storytelling, and play, and more than doubled a horse's natural life. Just as horses have banded together for protection and solidarity, we urge women to unite, because within humanity, we see women as prey and men as predators. If women band together, they can be a strong force in the effort to reconnect with Mother Earth.

"Some of our ancestors refused to alter their behavior. They continued to browse on shrubs and to live independently. Some survived for many generations, but as the forests continued to shrink, some of our closest cousins disappeared forever. Other herbivores followed our example, which increased their life expectancy as well. Should I slow down?"

"I'm okay. Please continue."

I wrote furiously to keep up with my new teacher. Sitting on the ground, encircled by a wall of legs, I felt like a foal secure within the family. The lead stallion, Cash, stood outside the circle and watchfully surveyed the field.

"On firmer ground, Dawn taught her children how to balance and run on their biggest toe, which made them run faster and maneuver quicker. The nail on that big toe developed into a hoof. Please look at the inside of my front leg above the knee. That rough, hairless spot of skin was a toe millions of years ago. We have another remnant toe near the joint just above the hoof.

"As millions of years passed, equines continued to grow taller and run faster. With the protection of the herd, our ancestors' horizons expanded. Horses could range further in a day than any other land animal. In a week, they could cover hundreds of miles. Equines spread from North America to South America, crossed the Bering Strait over a land bridge that once connected Alaska to Russia, and raised families in Asia, Europe, and Africa.

"Horses were selective of the grasses they ate and left plenty for others, but when seasons changed or drought came, they were the first to migrate to greener pastures or a fresh source of water. Other grazers, including antelope, wildebeest, bison, and other herding herbivores, soon followed. The carnivores followed too; the peril of predators kept the family bands closer together.

"Most of the time, horses successfully outran the meat-eaters, but when young or older equines could not keep up with the family, they became isolated and easy prey. The fatality rate of the young was very high. Sadly, half of the foals were lost in their first days of life. The loss of a family member or friend has always been a devastating experience. Generally, the band could not stay and mourn or they too would become a predator's meal. It's a dilemma we have struggled with for many generations.

"The Equus family included zebras, asses, onagers, horses, and the extinct quaggas. The physical differences between us evolved due to the adaptations we made to the local environments in which we lived. Yet we are all related and consider each other cousins."

"What is a quagga?"

"The friendly quaggas lived in the southern part of Africa. They had stripes similar to zebras on their head, neck, and chest; their bodies, flanks, and rear legs were a solid dun color, like a horse. They tried domestication a few hundred years ago when the Europeans arrived, but were shot into extinction.

"The remaining equines are so closely related we can interbreed. You call the offspring of a male ass, or donkey, and a female horse, a mule. A male horse and a female donkey's progeny is a hinny. A male zebra and a female horse give birth to a zebroid. A male zebra and a female ass produce a zebrass. On rare occasions, a male horse and a female mule create a hule, and a male ass and a female mule produce a jule. These are names that humans have assigned to particular equine offspring. The point we want to make is that we are all close, and when we say horses, we mean all members of the equine family. Our evolution took millions of years, but conscious choices brought us to this point," stated Bess.

"Conscious choices? Horses think about these things?"

"Yes. As you learn our history, the concept of our awareness will become clear to you. Horses admire humans as a species, but some of the conscious choices people have made, such as creating complex societies, have distanced them from their innate intuitive nature. This has further disconnected humans from sensitivity to other beings.

"Most people misinterpret other species' communications because they don't fit within the parameters of human speech. I don't mean to be condescending, but you must understand that much more communicating occurs than most humans perceive. All living beings—elephants, birds, cats, dogs, dolphins, and whales, to name a few—are connected and have thoughts and feelings. We each speak, or sing, our own song and understand some of our friends' languages. Often we use the senses of touch, taste, sight, and smell to communicate, but it is all conscious conversation. Since humans tend to isolate themselves on an island of superiority, people need to study the signs and signals of other species to re-learn how they talk. Humans once knew how to respect the Earth and connect with animals, but that has essentially been forgotten.

"Many animals have helped humans throughout history, but usually that help has gone unnoticed, or is considered just good luck. People judge most creatures by human standards, with no regard to the validity of other ways of communing and being. Only rarely have people recognized animal intelligence. Maybe, as you write our history, you can become an example of the potential humans have to develop more awareness of their own natural abilities.

"That knowledge will help you know yourself better, communicate with other humans more effectively, and sensitize you to other species as cognitive, feeling beings. Such an awareness will make people realize that all life on this planet is interrelated, which will help humans restore the Earth's balance."

"How do you know this?" I asked.

"We constantly talk amongst ourselves and teach the young our stories, which some are learning from me today. Plus, we share stories and news from horses and other beings around the world. Equines live close to nature and understand the need to survive, while preserving the environment for future generations. I understand your doubts about what I'm saying. You need to meet other equines in distant lands and learn from them also. Those equines will demonstrate that we are sentient beings making conscious choices. But please be patient, trust us, and be open; let us lead you for now. Our history takes time to tell. First, we would like you to meet some semi-wild ponies."

"Are mustangs semi-wild?"

"Almost all wild horses are feral, which means they or their ancestors were once domestic. Mustangs and other feral ponies living on open range would be very hard for you to approach and commune with, but there is a feral herd of ponies living on Kefalonia, an island off the coast of Greece, that we want you to meet."

Shaking my head at this serendipitous occurrence, I mused, "I've been planning a trip to Greece."

"That ancient land is filled with horse, as well as human, history. The semi-wild ponies there are famous. Spend as much time as possible with the horses and learn from them. Many Greeks know about the ponies; all you have to do is ask. Once you are in their mountain home, if you are calm, composed, and prove to be trustworthy, they will share their story.

"Remember: You will need a great deal of patience, because people are not allowed to approach, or touch, the prized ponies. Just try to telepathically connect and commune with them and observe how they live."

"Are there any wild horses left?"

"Unfortunately, the only large herds of truly wild horses are zebras. You have to go to Africa for their story; a zoo will not do."

"You want me to go to Africa?"

"Yes. Once you have spoken with the Kefalonian ponies and the zebras, you will have a new understanding and appreciation for equine roots and reasoning."

What an amazing day! One by one, I thanked the horses. Bess came last. For some unknown reason, I was crying. She brushed a tear from my cheek, wrapped her neck around me in understanding, and nickered with urgency, "Please travel safely and return soon."

"*I believe that horses are a doorway to our own humanity and spirituality in a way that is extraordinary and unique.*"

- Elizabeth Kaye McCall

SEMI-WILD PONIES
The Ainos Ponies; Kefalonia, Greece

Greece consists of a mainland and more than a thousand islands. The surrounding seas, a spectacular rainbow of blues, from the crystal clear, shallow shoreline to the midnight blue depths, contrast sharply with the rocky countryside. Located off the west coast of mainland Greece, Kefalonia is the largest of the Ionian Islands.

The travel agent at the Athens airport, who organized my lodging and transportation, knew of the prized ponies. She also arranged a meeting with Nikki Katsouni, the curator of the Museum of Natural History on Kefalonia. Nikki, a native, knew the island intimately, and had photographed the sacred ponies.

Upon arrival on the island, I met Nikki, who explained that the horses lived on the shoulder of Ainos Mountain, towering five thousand feet above the sea. For centuries, it served as a landmark for mariners traveling ancient shipping routes. The natural resources, fir forests for boat building, and beautiful beaches, contributed to the island's long history of human habitation.

Nikki arranged for Stavaros, a son of the major sheepherder on the mountain, to be my guide, and for Eleni, a bilingual native, to be my interpreter.

The next morning, Eleni and I drove up a narrow road carved into the side of Ainos. The road was so steep, it felt as though we were ascending in an airplane. The countryside dropped away; my ears popped. Several steep switchbacks later, we arrived at our meeting spot, Arginia, a quaint mountain village. The whitewashed homes were adorned with purple and yellow flowers. In the center of town, under the shade of a massive oak, burbled a freshwater spring. A locked lid protected the precious fresh water source.

From Arginia, we followed Stavaros up the mountain for several miles. The air was delightfully cool. Olive and oak trees grew among the hawthorn and strawberry bushes; short grasses, cacti, and small white and violet flowers held tenuous footholds in thin crevices.

I had to concentrate on my driving, and could not fully appreciate the panoramic vistas until we entered the horses' habitat and stopped at a rainwater collection tank. At two thousand feet above the sea, we could see coves and beaches stretching along the southern shoreline back to my bungalow, a forty-five-minute drive away. Below us lay groves of olive trees and fields of grapes and grains. The storage tank was one of only two sources of fresh water for the ponies and for Stavaros' goats. Above it, a concave concrete dish funneled rainwater into the tank. After filling the bone-dry trough, we continued slowly up the steep mountain.

At the crest of a rocky ridge a sign indicated the Zoodochos Pigi (Life Giver) Monastery, built in a small flat area adjacent to the only live spring on this side of the mountain. The monastery had been uninhabited for many years.

As we left our cars, Stavaros whispered and Eleni translated, "They are here for you. It is unusual; they are very shy around strangers." Less than a hundred yards away were several of the cherished horses. Delighted, I greeted the ponies and reassured them that we intended no harm, only love.

Three adult horses and a dark brown foal grazed contentedly. We walked quietly into the monastery's courtyard and sat on a bench under a huge oak tree. We neither moved nor spoke for several minutes as we observed the ponies and absorbed the beautiful scenery. To our left a narrow green valley stretched to the sea; Ainos Mountain loomed above, and the horses grazed peacefully just a few steps away. When we did talk, we spoke in whispers.

The largest of the three adults of this family band was a dapple-gray lead stallion who stood nearly fourteen hands high; a second, smaller stallion had a mottled brown coat; the third adult was an older gray mare, possibly pregnant. The dark brown foal was displaying its youthful exuberance by galloping in tight circles. The lead stallion kept a close eye on his foal. As the day warmed, the ponies moved into the shade of a large tree.

Stavaros explained, via Eleni, that horses were brought here in ancient times to log trees. Later the ponies helped with crop harvesting. To produce olive oil, horses pulled a single, round, crushing stone across a flat stone to press the "liquid gold" out of the olives. Stavaros then pointed to an ancient stone circle, approximately thirty feet across with a lipped rim. Masons had fitted the stones without mortar to keep the grains clean. Wheat was placed in the circle, and a pony would crush it with its hooves. To this day, nothing grew between many of the tightly laid stones.

In the past, the island's farmers allowed the horses to fend for themselves because they had no natural predators, and it was easier to let them graze in the wild than to build barns or stables and supply water and feed. During harvest season, villagers would tempt the horses with sweet grains, use them to process crops, and release the ponies when the work was finished. In winter, if it were unusually cold or heavy snow fell, the villagers would put out food for the horses. No fences have ever confined the steeds.

Tragically, in 1953, a major earthquake damaged or destroyed nearly every building on the island. The local economy was devastated; the human population declined precipitously, and the horses have not worked for humans since.

Most of the fir forests are gone now. The sprawling development to accommodate sun-worshipping beach lovers exemplifies a rapidly changing, fragile environment for the horses and the island. Occasionally, tourists come to take pictures if they are lucky enough to catch a glimpse of the horses. Stavaros and the other shepherds try to protect the ponies from human abuse. Since the island has changed so dramatically for the locals, the ponies represent a link to the ancient past.

The horses leisurely grazed in the shade. Then as Stavaros prepared to leave, a shiny black stallion appeared from behind the monastery. The dapple-gray lead stallion moved swiftly to confront him. After standing motionlessly nose to nose for several minutes, they both made stud piles. Each inspected the other's pile and again stood silently. Suddenly, they reared simultaneously and shadowboxed, but landed no direct blows. The seemingly choreographed confrontation ended quickly, the dispute resolved. The black stallion retreated behind the monastery; the dapple-gray returned to his family.

Stavaros said, "Bravo, Hal, you are lucky. I've lived with these horses all my life, and that is the first time I've seen them square off like that."

I asked Stavaros for permission to visit the horses on my own. He asked about my work and laughed at my response. He agreed and said he would inform the shepherds about my mission. Eleni and I lingered to watch the family of four. The lead stallion proudly pranced and played with his foal.

As we were about to leave, another band of horses emerged from behind the monastery. A dark gray stallion led; an older white mare with a limp was second; a dark brown foal followed. A light brown yearling was fourth, followed by a pale gray stallion. Bringing up the rear was the midnight black steed that had confronted the dapple-gray.

Eleni mused, "Stavaros was right, you are lucky. I've never seen two families at once."

Although less than one hundred yards apart, they remained separate. Slowly, the larger family grazed its way up the mountain and disappeared among the rocks. The other band slowly ambled behind the monastery to take a drink.

As we drove down the mountain, Eleni pointed out Arginia and noted that less than half of the homes were occupied. Some were used only a few weeks a year;

others were in various stages of disrepair. Since most of the mountain villages on the island were in similar poor condition, Eleni feared for their future. The lack of human life in Arginia was evident: I saw only one person during the ten days I passed through town.

During dinner, the native waiter told me that he had visited the monastery several times but had never had a glimpse of the horses. I retired early, filled with hope that my luck would continue.

Back at the rainwater collection tank the next day, movement on the hillside caught my eye. I unsuccessfully scanned the rocks for several minutes. Then, something moved: a gray mare and her foal. Perfectly camouflaged when standing still, they ascended and disappeared among the rocks.

Cresting the ridge above the monastery, I was engulfed by a herd of goats. Many were collared with bells that droned a slow innocuous tune in time with their pace. The goats had long, straight hair of varying earth tones; some had horns. They sure footedly ambled over the rock-strewn terrain and some maneuvered into seemingly impossible positions among the crags to avoid the sun.

The monastery was wrapped in undisturbed silence except for the goats' fading bells. A huge oak tree shaded the area around the spring that flowed from the rock wall on which the monastery was built. The water level in the full trough was maintained by a float value. Goat and horse droppings were everywhere. I left a few cut carrots for the ponies and returned to the monastery's courtyard.

Movement on the horizon caught my attention. I looked up and was blinded by a brilliant light. Shading my eyes, I fumbled for my sunglasses, and then realized that I was wearing them. The light shimmered and began to take form—it was a horse!

Light seemed to emanate from within the mare as if she were charged with electricity. When she walked into the shade, it was as though the current had been turned off. Back in the direct sunlight, her incandescent brightness returned. She seemed surreal, out of this world, like a goddess. When her angle to the sun changed, the light vanished, and the mare's limp, seen the previous day, became evident. I suspect that similar visions have been the basis of many a myth or legend.

The rest of the family now appeared in the same order as the previous day. They sauntered down the road to drink at the trough. I watched motionlessly from less than fifty feet away. The midnight black lead stallion was last. He and the mare contrasted perfectly in color, as well as in disposition. He was clearly the protector: the most vocal and haughty, yet the most aware of everyone and everything in his domain. He tolerated me because I showed no aggressive movement and was simply content to observe.

Nor did the lead mare indicate any objection to my presence. She was also very perceptive, but subdued and docile due to her injury. In fact, she moved closer to me and presented her injured left foreleg, which was quite swollen at the ankle. Putting weight on it obviously caused her pain, yet she showed more concern for her baby than the impairment. If the injury did not heal properly, this foal might be her last.

Twice the foal left the mare to dash around the courtyard at amazing speed. Its young legs—too big for its body—seemed to carry the foal beyond its capability, and it often stopped to wonder at its own agility, only to turn and sprint at full speed again. The colt joined the foal in a follow-the-leader running game. As swift as the little foal was, the yearling was faster, and playfully pulled the foal's mane. The dark and light gray stallions meanwhile assumed protective positions around the mare and took turns grazing. The mare stood motionless on her three healthy legs. From the cover of a small tree, the midnight black stallion watched everything.

I hardly moved except to turn my head to observe the horses. The cover of a tree provided respite from the heat of the sun. The mare hobbled painfully uphill towards shade for her family.

Driving down the mountain, I was already envisioning seeing the horses the next day. I wanted to stay overnight on the mountain to be closer to the ponies, but Stavaros had cautioned me that people had been robbed. Also, no camping was allowed in the National Park that bordered the horses' home.

The next morning, translucent cirrus clouds floated high in the sky. The trees cast long shadows as my "plane" headed up the mountain for the horses' home. At two thousand feet, the air was crisp, clean, and cool. In summer, the temperature may rise into the nineties before noon.

At the monastery, no horses or goats were about. Nature's calming silence lent a sense of security to the environs until an odd knocking sound, coming from a tall tree, broke the spell. With my binoculars, I located a large woodpecker with black plumage and a bright red crown. It flew off, and as I followed its flight, four ponies came into my view. They were a bachelor band and may have been brothers. They had the same body conformation, were graduated in size, and were completely midnight black. They appeared timid compared to the family bands. The three smallest huddled together; the fourth, acting like a lead stallion, circled their perimeter. He approached within thirty feet of me and made a stud pile to establish my boundary.

The bachelor band then slowly ascended a rocky hill. I returned to the water trough to discover the untouched treats and realized that the semi-wild ponies had never seen a carrot.

The following day I brought crisp green apples and hoped for better results. After no horses appeared in more than an hour, I started to descend the mountain. On the last ridge above the rainwater collection tank, three horses grazed.

This group was another bachelor band. The two larger horses looked like brothers: both had light gray coats. The smallest of the three inched cautiously closer. The other two, startled by my presence, quickly vanished. The largest one soon returned to summon the curious youngster, who reluctantly turned away and followed his leader out of sight.

I had read that bands of wild horses usually consist of one stallion, several mares, plus yearlings and foals. Of the seventeen ponies I'd seen thus far, thirteen were males, three were females, and three were foals. The ratio was disproportionate. I was also concerned that none of the wild horses had talked with me the way Bess had. Was I missing their communication? Doubt crept into my mind about my ability to communicate with horses.

As I left the horses' home early in the day, I decided to go to Fiscardo, the island's northernmost town and home to the Fiscardo Nautical and Environmental

Club (FNEC) to visit their horses. FNEC is a nonprofit foundation attempting to preserve, protect, and rescue the island's fragile ecosystems from damage caused by people. I arrived at its headquarters just as a woman was unlocking the door.

"Calle merda (good morning)," I offered in my best Greek.

She responded in an English accent that ensured I would not have to struggle to communicate. Stacy was one of the project coordinators and the woman I had spoken to when inquiring about the FNEC horses. She invited me to visit the museum while she filled a container of water in the back of a pickup truck for them. The educational information about the land and the sea was impressively presented, and graphically demonstrated the extensive human pollution of the last century.

At the paddock, Stacy introduced me to their horses; three were Haflingers from Germany, one was Greek, reminiscent of the Ainos ponies. The horses were to be used for fire patrolling on the mountain to help preserve the environment. Horses ecologically impact the terrain less than motorized vehicles, they cause no air pollution, and they leave manure that fertilizes the land.

Since Stacy had to leave, she introduced me to Jodee, a new volunteer from Canada. Jodee had grown up with horses and had ridden since she was seven. She was constructing a wooden lean-to to provide shade for the four horses. A passing car sprayed gravel into the paddock. The horses pinned their ears back and retreated to the far side of the enclosure. I told Jodee the horses were not happy to be near the road.

She said that a larger paddock with sufficient grass, easy access to water, room to roam, and far from the noisy road, would be ready in a couple of weeks. The horses listened intently to Jodee's words and relaxed. Their ears perked in my direction when I mentioned carrots.

Jodee tied the horses separately before they were fed, because they had food issues. The Haflingers had arrived two weeks earlier and the little pony only a few days ago. I sensed his insecurity of being outnumbered by the others. After securing the Haflingers, Jodee chased after the white pony.

The first Haflinger, Luna, was broad and very healthy. She sniffed me, and I offered her a carrot while stroking her beautiful chestnut coat. Luna welcomed me as she crunched the carrot and asked, "Are we going for a ride?" I was startled: this was the first horse to talk to me on the island.

"No, I am just visiting," I answered mentally.

"Do you have enough carrots for everyone?" Luna questioned as the other two Haflingers looked over their shoulders.

"Yes, there's plenty for all," I laughed, and observed Jodee still chasing the pony, whose ribs plainly showed through her thin coat.

Next I turned to Enzo, a gelding who was bigger and broader than Luna. He had a white stripe on his face and a pink-tipped nose. I offered him a carrot that he savored in small bites. He also nickered a welcome and asked, "Are you sure you aren't taking us riding? We'd love to get out of this paddock, stretch our legs, and see some of the island."

"No, I just wanted to say hi and to give you a treat," I responded.

Jodee took a break from chasing Astero ("Star" in Greek). I asked her if the horses had been ridden since their arrival, and commented that the Haflingers were restless. Jodee said that the staff had been very busy, but she would take them for a ride that afternoon. The horses neighed their gratitude.

Barbie was pawing the ground for a carrot before I approached. She nibbled it to make the treat last as long as possible. Beautiful Barbie, the shortest of the three, had a gorgeous, long, light-colored mane and bangs that partially covered her eyes. As I groomed her, I admired her creamy coat.

"You came here just to give us carrots?" Barbie asked happily.

"Actually, I traveled from America to meet the wild ponies here, but I haven't had any luck communicating with them."

Barbie said that the mountain horses were quite shy because humans were unpredictable. Some people respected the wild ponies, but some were cruel. She explained about kidnapping and shooting incidents.

"How do you know this?" I asked.

"Astero told us. Her mother, part of a family band on the mountain, was pregnant with Astero when she was kidnapped. Give Jodee a carrot for Astero. Then she will be easy to catch."

Barbie's advice succeeded: the skittish horse was under control in moments. She gleefully munched her treat. I inched forward with another. Her pinned-back ears indicated her wariness. The Haflingers whinnied reassurances. Astero nodded in gratitude, relaxed, and happily took her treat.

Jodee said that Astero had been difficult to manage. She had thrown one of the FNEC directors who had sustained a broken arm.

After another carrot, Astero began to relate her past mistreatment. She had had several different owners; some had treated her badly. At her last home, she was separated from her mother, was underfed, and had very little contact with other horses or humans. Astero was also confused about what to expect from her new home. She said that one of the few good things about people was the carrots they gave as treats. She could not get enough of them.

Then Astero said, "Just after I arrived at this place, with no formal greeting, a man jumped on my back and kicked me in the sides. Startled, I reared. The man fell off and hurt his arm. If he had been gentle in his approach, taken his time, everything would have been fine. But he reminded me of a man who had beaten me, and I was frightened."

I stroked her neck as she munched another carrot. I reassured her that her new home was safe. I would tell her guardians to be gentle and patient. She wrapped her head and neck around me and gave me a huge horse hug. I absorbed the love she gave and returned her embrace.

Thoroughly calm, Astero asked where I was from and why I was there.

I told her my mission.

Astero laughed and asked, "Did you try to give them carrots?"

"Yes, but I had no luck. Today I left apples. Will they like them?"

Astero whispered that the wild ponies had never seen carrots or apples, but would love long fresh-cut grass. "My mother once roamed the mountain before she and several other mares were taken away by people. My mother was pregnant with me when she was captured. But I would love to roam the mountain and see my cousins."

"If you are good to the people here, they will use you on the mountain to patrol for fires, and you might have a chance to see your family."

"That would be great!" Astero said.

She shook her head, laid it on my shoulder, and requested another carrot. I gladly complied. When Jodee joined us, she mused that this was the first time that she had seen Astero show affection. I gently rubbed Astero's ears and explained that she would be a different pony now. I told her that Astero was looking forward to patrolling the mountain and gave Jodee the rest of the carrots. I had finally communicated with horses on Kefalonia! I was filled with hope.

It was still dark the next morning when I left for the horses' home. Discovering some fresh-cut grass along the side of the road, I scooped up enough to fill the passenger side of the car.

At the monastery's water trough lay the uneaten apples. I sat in the shade and waited for the ponies. After several hours, I became discouraged and disappointedly drove down the mountain.

As I crested the ridge near the rainwater tank, I spotted a light gray stallion playing tag with a brown foal. One moment the stallion led the foal, but as soon as the foal touched the stallion's flank, the action reversed. The foal tried fruitlessly to out run the stallion. The stallion nipped at the foal's neck then turned and ran away as the foal stopped and pivoted to chase the stallion. Fast and very light on their feet, father and child dashed back and forth across the open field with total abandon.

The game of tag continued for several more minutes as three other horses, heedless of the frolicking, lazily grazed into view. Two were stallions, smaller and lighter in color than the playful stallion. The smaller of the two had a white nose. The third horse, a dark gray mare with a pink nose and rounded belly, looked pregnant. Their long tails had the same coloring: gray at the top flowing into gold.

They noticed me, but paid little attention except for an occasional glance. With an armful of grass, I walked slowly toward the ponies. They all looked at me intently. I stopped, laid the grass in piles, and retreated. The three adult horses continued grazing, but the lead stallion left the foal with the others, meandered to a pile of grass, and sniffed it casually. He glanced about, nibbled a mouthful, chewed it, and took another.

Suddenly, the family band stopped and stood at attention. The lead stallion rejoined his family and assumed a defensive position between his band and the bachelor band that appeared on the horizon. The lead stallion approached the bachelors, vocalized a warning, and ushered his band toward me. After a few steps, he turned, lowered his head, and charged. The bachelors scattered.

A crisis averted, the family band munched the grass offering and edged closer to me. As they passed, I heard the mare whinny, "Thank you."

Stunned, I softly said, "You're welcome."

With the bachelors at a safe distance, the stallion trotted to the fresh-cut grass for another bite. Turning toward me, he shook his head, expressed his thanks, and muttered that the bachelors were always trying to steal a female. He said that he felt sorry for them, because there were so few mares.

Thanks to Astero and the Haflingers, I had finally established a connection with the Ainos ponies.

The next day, after passing the rainwater tank, I spotted the same bachelor band of four black horses. Ascending further, I heard the goats' music permeating the air. Goats were everywhere—they crowded around the drinking trough and encircled the monastery. One was devouring a cactus with sharp thorns down to a nub. Goats could quickly strip an area of vegetation if the shepherds were lax in herding them. No horses were present, so I headed back down the mountain.

Near the lower water tank grazed the bachelor band. All four lifted their heads to eye me curiously. I immediately stopped the car and turned off the engine. The horses resumed grazing. I shifted the car into neutral so I could silently follow them downhill until we were just fifteen feet apart.

Less than a hundred feet away, the family of three gray stallions, the gray mare, and her foal stood at the drinking trough. The bachelor band crossed the road and edged closer to the trough. The family took a defensive position behind the trough, with two stallions flanking the mare, and the lead stallion nudging the foal further away. The bachelor band boldly advanced toward the mare. When her flanking stallions screamed a warning, the bachelors halted.

Moving as a unit, the bachelors tried to approach the trough. The lead stallion stepped forward to block them. He made a stud pile that separated the two groups, now standing less than twenty feet apart. The bachelors hesitated, but then were distracted by the family band that I had seen the first day coming up the road. A dark gray stallion was leading; the once incandescently bright white limping mare was second, followed by her foal, the brown colt, and the light gray stallion. The midnight black leader was protecting the rear.

Sensing an opportunity to either gain control of the water source or to steal the mare, the bachelor band edged closer. The two gray stallions and the mare huddled tightly together, but didn't budge.

The black stallion's family moved into the position that the bachelors had just vacated. An intense stare-down ensued as fifteen of the fabled ponies performed negotiations that have been practiced for countless generations.

The mare at the trough broke the hypnotic spell; she lay down, rolled onto her back, displayed her pregnant belly for all to see, and then stood again. The bachelor band edged closer to the mare. Her lead black stallion stepped forward and screamed.

The lead gray stallion pushed his foal to the far side of a tree for safety and approached the black leader. They stood nose to nose for several seconds then tossed their heads back and forth communicating silently. The black stallion made a stud pile; the gray responding with one of his own. They read each other's droppings and stood close enough to whisper. Then the black stallion inspected the water trough. When he was satisfied, he ambled back to the gray leader. The black stallion then yelled to his family. They turned their backs on the other horses, but stood flank to flank, creating a formidable defense.

When the two stallions and mare retreated from the trough, the bachelors inched forward. The black leader returned to the water and screamed at the bachelors to no avail. The two stallions with the mare did not flinch. Finally, the black stallion leaped over the trough and chased the bachelor band across a field.

Meanwhile, the black stallion's family proceeded slowly uphill toward the shade of a large tree to wait. The black leader returned and snorted a gesture of appreciation to the gray stallion's family. The undaunted bachelors regrouped and edged closer while pretending to feed. The gray leader signaled his foal to join her mother between the two stallions. The gray's family then turned away and proceeded down the road.

The gray leader remained by the water trough for several more minutes before calling to his family. They stopped and waited. Without taking any water, he jumped over the trough and chased the bachelors further down the hill until they disappeared from view. The gray stallion then returned to his band.

As it turned out, the trough was almost dry, so there was not enough water for all the horses. The ponies had determined the order in which each family would drink, and the band at the trough had relinquished their turn without taking any more for the sake of the others. The black stallion's family, having an injured mare, a foal, and a yearling were the next priority. The bachelors would have to wait their turn.

Before leaving, I filled the trough and heard a whinny of, "Thank you."

The wondrous drama would have made an award-winning documentary, because the ponies used conscious communication, sharing, and sacrifice to settle a dispute over a limited water source, without resorting to physical violence. The incident proved to me, once again, that horses are sentient beings who communicate in many ways.

The next morning, feeling melancholy about having to leave the island, I gathered grass and wondered whether I had missed any messages.

Near the rainwater tank, the familiar music of bells filled the air. Rounding the bend, I was engulfed by a huge herd of goats and drove slowly as they parted. I waved to the shepherd.

Beyond the ridge, the symphony faded. Horses, too far away to identify, drank and played at the monastery. I placed the grass next to the stone circle and took shelter from the sun under a small tree. A few minutes later, the horses emerged from behind the buildings.

A new family, led by a large dapple-gray mare, approached in single file. The first two ponies were mares, the second one slightly smaller and darker than the first. Her rounded belly implied that she was pregnant. A small, light brown foal followed the mares; last came a dark brown colt. They paraded right past me and began eating the fresh grass. This was the first time I had seen a band with more than one mare. Blissfully, I watched the family graze, when I noticed a stallion standing over me.

He said, "Thanks for the grass; it's appreciated. With so many goats, it's difficult to find enough food. Sometimes, the grasses are so short we cannot nibble them. Then we go hungry."

"You're welcome," was all I could manage.

The mares continued to graze while the colt and foal romped in circles around the field. A frisky game of tag ensued. The young horses never faltered, even on rocky ground. Their play was joyful. This family band appeared the healthiest of the herd: all were well fed, and their coats had a lustrous sheen.

Intent on watching the colt and foal frolic, I had forgotten the stallion standing beside me. We now shared the shade of a single tree. He intently watched his youngsters play, and the mares graze, as he protectively scanned the field.

While I tried to think of something intelligent to say, he began, "Why are you here?"

"A horse named Bess asked me to write a book about horses using your words. She said that I should meet the wild Ainos ponies."

"Really, we are only semi-wild. Long ago, we were brought here by men to work, but now we live virtually on our own. Sadly, we may soon disappear."

"Why?"

"You've been coming here for many days. I've watched you from afar and have spoken with other horses. I thought you knew our desperate situation. How many ponies have you seen?"

"Twenty-seven total: six mares, seventeen stallions, and four foals."

"We are out of balance. There are too few females. How can we survive? Living and working on the island has been a blessing and a curse. At first, there were no natural predators, and we frequently roamed free. New horses arrived periodically, which was critical for keeping us healthy, but that stopped long ago.

Several herds once lived on the mountain, now there is only one. Our future survival completely depends on people. If new mares are not brought here, we will die out in a few generations!

"Humans are also out of balance. They must learn to respect and value each other and the Earth, or humanity will face its own ruin."

Stomping the ground vehemently, he declared, "ALL FEMALES ARE PRECIOUS—THEY ARE OUR MOTHERS, SISTERS, AND DAUGHTERS. THEY ARE THE NURTURERS OF THE WORLD. THE PRESERVATION OF LIFE ON EARTH IS DEPENDENT UPON THEM!

"To us, humans are an enigma. Some are kind and caring, but some are incredibly cruel. People must learn to appreciate females and all that life has to offer."

After writing his words, I looked up. The family band had disappeared as a carload of tourists rumbled up the road. I turned to the stallion, but he too had vanished.

The empty expanse, now devoid of the prized ponies, sizzled in the midday sun.

"The greatness of a nation and its moral progress can be judged by the way its animals are treated."

- GANDHI

WILD HORSES

Zebras; Mashatu Game Reserve, Botswana

Z ebras live in many places throughout Africa. I chose to visit the Mashatu Game Reserve in Botswana, because its national seal displays two rearing zebras, and the one pula coin is graced with the galloping striped steed.

Botswana, a landlocked country located in southern Africa, is proactive about animal and land conservation. Almost a fifth of the country is designated as national park land; another fifth is under constant government wildlife management. Several private companies have developed ecotourism and community-based conservation programs, which limit the number of visitors to minimize the stress on the animals and the land. As a result, game watching is enhanced and the country remains virtually pristine. The Mashatu Game Reserve is one of the protected preserves.

The Limpopo River, the "great greasy green" that Kipling had made renowned more than a century before, serves as the eastern boundary of Mashatu and the border between Botswana and South Africa. This woodland savanna is comprised of wide-open spaces with thick vegetation lining the riverbanks.

The airport, with no town in sight, consists of a small landing strip and an oversized thatched hut. George, a representative from Mashatu, stood beside a Land Cruiser that had no doors or top and greeted me with a broad smile. The rough ride, on dirt track through open land dotted with low bushes and sparse trees, took about an hour. The ground was bare except for patches of dry grass; the seasonal spring rains had yet to arrive. Near the campground, a herd of impalas lazed in the shade.

Clare, one of the managers, showed me around the camp. We crossed the lush, landscaped courtyard. Irrigation made this area an oasis of manicured grass and bushes. A covered, open-air meeting and dining area overlooked a waterhole created for the animals. To the left was a bar, "The Gin Trap," and to the right were indoor and outdoor wildlife viewing areas. Numerous birds called from around the waterhole. Clare said that Mashatu was an ornithologist's dream: more than three hundred species of birds had been spotted on the reserve.

Nearby, the "Discovery Room" was filled with informative displays. An elephant totem pole tracked elephants' ages by their height, since elephants continue to grow well past the age of forty. The reserve promised to be an excellent educational experience, because it had an archeologist and an elephant ecologist onsite, and most of the staff were locals.

A dozen huts surrounded the main courtyard. A photograph of a zebra hung over the bed in the hut assigned to me. The other lodges had pictures of lions, leopards, and elephants, but mine was the only one with a zebra. Just outside my door stood an eight-inch-tall baby steenbok, whose mother left him in camp for protection during the day, and came to nurse at night.

The food at Mashatu was delicious. Small, cute, tan and gray Vervet monkeys with white hairy chests never missed a meal. They used their long tails as a fifth limb to hang from branches. The monkeys were quick to take advantage of any opportunity to snatch snacks. The continuous game between the servers, trying to protect the food, and the monkeys, trying to steal a prize, was a constant source of entertainment.

After the heat of the day passed, I went on my first game-watching excursion. Ben, our spotter, was waiting at the vehicle and introduced himself. He was a friendly, smiling local who had a potbelly and a firm handshake. Ben had lost his left arm in an accident when he was a child.

Catherine and Debbie from South Africa joined us. Moments later, a tall, lean man with a rifle approached the Land Cruiser just as the two-way radio mounted to the dashboard crackled, "God, God, are you there, God?"

The man placed the gun in its rack above the dashboard and waited a long, silent moment. He turned to us, and with a broad, beaming smile, answered, "This is Godfrey. May I help you?"

We laughed when we realized that this scene had been played out many times. Still it was a comfort to know that we had "God" for a guide.

Ben sat high in the spotter's seat at the rear of the vehicle. Godfrey carefully navigated us around the reserve on unpaved tracks. We spotted more than twenty impala and four kudu, their larger cousins with four-foot antlers that spiraled up and out. They were as big as North American elk. We encountered the largest and smallest relatives of the impala: the enormous eland and the very small steenbok. Ben said that the bull eland could weigh up to a ton and have two-foot-long straight swirled horns. He added that the steenbok had no antlers and mated for life.

On the way to one of Godfrey's favorite places, we slowed to observe four zebras. Wide-eyed, I gasped, enthralled with their close proximity and striking beauty. Ben said two types of zebras lived in southern Africa: the rare Grebbie Zebra, on the verge of extinction, and the larger Plains Zebra, which grazed beside us. Apart from the stripes and stiff, upright manes, the zebras' conformation reminded me of the Ainos ponies. Their stripes extended down the bellies, around the legs, and ended as short black socks above the hooves. The stripes continued up the neck and around the face. The zebras had large dark eyes and long twitching ears that swiveled independently. Their three-foot-long tails ended in a tuft of black hair. One by one, they drifted into the brush.

We stopped at a popular waterhole, in an otherwise dry riverbed, which was protected by the shade of several gigantic, deciduous Nyala trees. Godfrey said that this spot never dried, even in the worst drought. More than a dozen impala mingled around the water, a black-backed jackal observed from the bank above, a six-foot crocodile sunned himself on a log, and two fish eagles lurked in the trees. A few feet from the water, a mother elephant was teaching her two daughters how to create a well. Ben explained that elephants liked to drink fresh water and dug wells just slightly larger than their trunks. During droughts, many animals depended upon the elephants' wells for water.

When we left the drinking spot, we clung to the vehicle as it climbed the steep riverbank. In the distance lounged a small pride of lions. We parked incredibly close and were mesmerized by them. Two mothers lazed in the shade while three small, feisty cubs romped around them. Lions, the only social cats that live in groups, or prides, sleep up to eighteen hours a day and hunt primarily at night.

We proceeded to a nearby hill for a bird's-eye view of the plain and to watch the sun set. The panorama of the orange-tinted sky above, and the vast open plain below, was breathtakingly majestic. A cumulus cloud cluster to the east, and a spectacular lightning display on the horizon, portended rain, but only a few drops reached the dry, dusty ground. Minutes later, a glowing bright rainbow arched across the eastern sky.

That evening, while contemplating the day's visual wonders, I was overcome with a sense of urgency to commune with the abundant wildlife of this magical haven.

Godfrey woke me in the pre-dawn darkness at five o'clock the next morning. Fifteen minutes later the sun had risen. The sweet scent of wild sage wafted around us. Ben pointed out the large Mashatu tree for which the reserve was named and said that its intertwined trunks had a circumference of more than double its fifty-foot height.

This early excursion would be Catherine and Debbie's last. Since they especially wanted to see big cats, I sent a mental message of love and peace to our feline friends. Just a few minutes from camp, under the shade of several trees, a large male leopard made a spectacular leap between branches. Ben said that a leopard might wait in one place all day for an unsuspecting impala.

We crossed a dry stream bed and found a big paw print. Ben told us that it belonged to the "King of the Savanna" and was less than thirty minutes old. We followed the tracks, and when we circled a stand of sickle bushes, there he was, lying in their shade. The large lion watched our approach. Godfrey drove slowly to within twenty feet. Amazingly, the huge, healthy, male lion, with a full sandy-colored mane that turned dark as it spread onto his chest and shoulders, remained relaxed. Ben estimated him to weigh more than five hundred pounds and be about eight years old. His paws were as wide as my two fists together. We were close enough to hear his panted breathing.

On the return to camp, we passed several elephant families browsing on trees. Ben whispered to Godfrey in Setswana. We stopped near a low rocky mound out of which grew a single, leafless tree. Catherine gasped when a sleek cheetah stepped calmly from behind a bush and slowly ambled away. I mentally told the cheetah that she was safe; we would not harm her.

She turned toward us, "You promise you're not going to hurt me?"

Stunned to hear her soft tone, I answered, "We promise."

She looked left and right, and then took several steps towards us before turning to display her elegant profile. The cheetah was lean and had a light tan coat with small black spots over her entire body except her chest, which was covered in soft, white hair. She had a long, thin, black-tipped tail that curved upward. She silently padded up the mound and sat facing us.

Godfrey commented that cheetahs were very shy; this was the first one he had seen in two months. Ben added that cheetahs were the swiftest land animal on Earth and could sprint faster than sixty miles per hour.

I asked the cheetah, "What is your favorite food?"

"Steenbok," she answered.

I asked Godfrey the same question. He thought it was impala.

I asked the cheetah, "Why steenbok?"

She responded, "They are small and have no protective antlers. When I take one for dinner, I can easily carry it to a safe place to enjoy it. Killing impala is much more dangerous, because they have horns and are considerably larger. Impalas are too big to carry, so I have to eat quickly before the scavengers arrive. Plus I could never eat a whole impala in a single meal." She added that talk of food had made her hungry. In a quick fluid movement, she disappeared down the other side of the hill.

Catherine marveled at having seen all of the savanna's big cats in one morning. I was thankful to hear the feline's words. Given all the predators in the area, it was no surprise that zebras were elsewhere.

The camp managers, aware of my desire to commune with zebras, scheduled Grant, the archeologist, and Isaac, a tracker, to take me out alone.

On the western side of the reserve, Grant had seen zebras the previous evening where many elephants milled about. Zebras like to stay near fresh water, and the Lalapanzi, a natural spring, was close by. Isaac said that relatively few zebras inhabited Mashatu in the early spring, because the arid land provided little nourishment. Grant added that within a week of the rain's onset, the barren plain would be transformed into a lush field of grass at its most nutritious stage. Then more than a thousand zebras would migrate to the reserve. Many of the females would be pregnant and would give birth just after the new grass sprouted, so they would have ample nourishment to produce milk for their young.

We parked among bushes next to a clearing. Across the dry riverbed, a dozen zebras grazed peacefully. One glanced in our direction. I immediately sent the zebras our love, told them we meant no harm, and that horses had sent me to speak with them.

All the zebras stopped grazing and looked at us intently. The stallion took a few steps forward, positioned himself between us and the other zebras, and without breaking eye contact, suspiciously said, "Why would horses send you to talk with us?"

"Horses asked me to write a book about equines. They sent me here to learn how horses lived for millions of years before domestication. It looks like you have a large healthy family," I said to compliment him.

"Nothing could be further from the truth," he responded gruffly. "We are in trouble!" He walked towards the six zebras to his right, lowered his head, and extended his nose. "These zebras are part of another family band. We came together to drink as there is safety in numbers, but since the land is dry and food is scarce, families usually have to graze separately." He retreated from his posturing position when another stallion appeared. The two stallions stood close together, faced each other, and touched nose to cheek as a greeting. After a few moments of head bobbing, the second stallion escorted his family down the riverbank.

"I do not have a large healthy family. I did, but not anymore," he said sadly.

"Why is that?" I asked.

"Because of man," he responded. "My family had three healthy adult females, two of whom were pregnant including our leader, the oldest and wisest mare. We had just completed our winter migration. The coming spring seemed promising. Recently, my lead lady was standing by my side when she suddenly fell to the ground dead as a loud crack thundered in my ears. Frightened, I quickly led my family away to a safe distance. All we could do was watch as three men came out of the bush in a vehicle like yours. They took only her skin and left her body for the vultures, which devoured her and my unborn daughter in just a few minutes."

"That's horrible. Were they hunting illegally?" I asked.

"Does it matter? She was gone, and we had no time to mourn. She was the most knowledgeable member in our family. She knew the locations of fresh water and all the migration routes. This information had been passed down for generations, but she had not yet taught the younger females all she knew. She also had much experience raising our young. This pregnancy was her fourth. Only one other female in our band has given birth. The stress of losing our lead female so violently caused my other pregnant lady to abort. Now we will have no new babies this year. Everyone is anxious. I am worried about keeping my family together. Whenever we lose a family member to predators, it is a sad occasion. But that usually happens to a baby or a weak individual we cannot defend. To lose the band's leading lady so senselessly is devastating. Hundreds of thousands of my kin have met the same fate, dying because man just wanted our striped skin for a trophy."

"I am sorry for your loss. What will you do?"

"We now move in a new order. Once I set the arrangement, which is determined by age, knowledge, and character, we practice defending ourselves by running and turning as a single unit. This skill is crucial for our survival, because it confuses predators, who have difficulty selecting the weakest individual from our continuous line of black and white. Since each zebra's markings are different, we also must retrain ourselves to recognize the unique line pattern we create, so we can quickly tell if a family member is missing. Later, when the rains come, and the herd gathers, we will try to learn water locations and migration routes from other families.

"Our loss has also left us with an odd number in the band. One member will feel isolated without having a best friend with whom to form a pair bond."

"What is a pair bond?"

"Pair bonds are two zebras that form a very close relationship through mutual caring and play. This helps make the family tighter."

"What will happen to the single zebra?"

"When the herd gathers, I will look for another lady to join us."

"What happens if you can't find one?"

"The single individual may wander off and join another band."

"Good luck in your search. Is there anything we can do?"

"I do not know. At times, everything seems absurd. I can smell that you have a gun. Are we safe from hunters here?"

I asked Grant whether hunting was permitted within Mashatu. He said no and added that within the reserve, no incidents had occurred for several years, but the zebras would be exposed to poachers if they crossed the Shashe River into Zimbabwe or the Limpopo River into South Africa.

The zebra thanked us for the information, and I reassured him that his family would be safe from humans within the boundaries of the two rivers. I also told him where we had found a large lion. The zebras bobbed their heads in acknowledgement. I thanked them for their time and patience.

Grant started the engine, and we slowly retreated into the bushes. We headed for a hill on the southern horizon for our afternoon break. I was elated to have finally spoken with zebras, but troubled by man's wanton slaughter of wildlife for trophies.

As we bumped along the dusty savanna, an enormous elephant approached and stopped behind a tree. He had large floppy ears and four-foot-long tusks. Grant turned off the engine. He estimated the bull to be more than forty years old, and one of the largest elephants he had ever seen. As soon as the motor's noise ceased, the large bull quickly moved around the tree to block our path. He could have reached out and touched us with his trunk.

Grant fearfully looked up at the elephant. He depressed the clutch and slowly shifted the vehicle into reverse without starting the engine. He said, "Elephant, you have my attention. I am a little wary of you."

The elephant laughed and said, "Sorry, I did not mean to frighten you. But are you here just to write about zebras, or will you tell our tale, too?"

Stunned, I answered, "I would be honored to write the elephants' story."

"Thank you," he responded and stepped aside.

I chuckled inwardly as the tension in Grant's face ebbed. He started the vehicle, shifted, and crept forward past the big bull. The elephant followed closely.

As Grant accelerated, so did the pachyderm, who called, "Please, do not forget to write about the elephants." After I repeated my promise, he slowed and veered away.

We drove to the top of a hill to watch the sun set. On the plain below, Grant spotted two zebras. I silently sent them a message of love and peace. While we watched the glowing sun slip below the horizon, the zebras edged closer. As night swiftly engulfed the plain, the zebras walked uphill to within a stone's throw of us. Grant thought this amazing, because zebras usually shied away from people. Isaac said that this was the closest he had ever been to wild zebras; Grant concurred. Before departing, I thanked the zebras for their trust and wished them well.

Our encounter with the massive elephant caused abundant laughter at dinner. Some of the staff wanted to learn how to telepathically communicate with animals. I explained that people have to learn to live in the moment to talk with another species.

Gregg, a manager, wondered whether he could use animal communication to help him take better wildlife photographs. He wanted to try it with the large lion that we had observed. I suggested that he begin by sending his love and telling the big cat that he would cause him no harm; he just wanted to take his picture.

The next day, Gregg had a great tale. He had found the large lion lying in the shade. Gregg greeted the lion with love and promised he would cause him no harm; he only wanted to take photographs. Gregg asked the lion if he would move into the sunlight. He was totally surprised when the lion rose, sat in the direct sun, and struck a perfect pose. Gregg took more pictures than he had ever taken in one session. He was thrilled to have connected with the cooperative lion.

Everyone expressed gratitude at sharing such a wondrous place with so many amazing animals. We vowed to try to live more within the moment and clearly communicate our thoughts. After dinner, the staff sang several traditional Setswana songs. Their beautiful a cappella harmonics filled the air. As the golden disk of the full moon rose in the sky, we told stories and laughed until after midnight. Yet I was inwardly sad that tomorrow would be my last game-viewing opportunity.

In the cool hour before sunrise, my eyes took a few moments to adjust to the dusky light. Two adult eland were leisurely grazing on the lush courtyard grass, and a warthog with three babies tumbled in the dirt. They were fortunate to live part of their lives in the protected confines of the camp.

Fiona, from England, was interested in my task and asked to join our group. I welcomed her company, but advised her that my only goal was to see zebras. She was amenable to that purpose and shyly confided that she had once spoken with a locust. Fiona thought that the locust was a beautiful creature and had told it so. She asked why it was so destructive. The locust had clearly responded, "Who is the real destructive one?"

Even though the rains had yet to arrive, the longer days signaled the trees to burst forth with life. Hundreds of impala browsed everywhere. Godfrey noted that the sixteen thousand impala on the reserve made a greater environmental impact than any other animal, including the elephants.

Since Fiona wanted to see the famed literary river, we headed towards the Limpopo. The riverbed was more than one hundred yards wide, but contained no flowing water, only disconnected pools. One could walk across the river without getting wet feet.

Godfrey pointed to the driftwood strewn atop the riverbanks. He said that two years before, heavy spring rains had flooded the Limpopo and deposited the wood. The flooding caused so much destruction that Mashatu Reserve had to close for six weeks.

Leaving the Limpopo, we spooked a family of wildebeests. When I sent a message of love to them, they stopped in the shade of the closest trees. The wildebeest, a large, cow-like antelope with short thick horns, can be extremely dangerous. Godfrey noted that they frequently grazed and migrated with zebras.

Heading slowly toward camp, Ben spotted fresh prints. Numerous tracks ran together and formed a path, but two pair ran parallel. One was an elephant's; a large oval pattern that left an impression in the ground bigger than a man's two feet. The second were unmistakably a zebra's print.

Further along, we met five elephants. A young female, with two-foot-long tusks, ambled in front of her mother. Godfrey estimated the mom to be about twenty-five years old. The elder daughter of the second adult was next. Following her was a cute little two-year-old, who already weighed more than five hundred pounds. Their large mother, replete with three-foot-long tusks, followed closely. Ben estimated her to be about thirty and speculated that the two adults might be sisters.

Four of the elephants crossed the trail in front of us, stopped on the far side, then turned and faced the remaining mother, who looked squarely at me and asked, "Are you only going to write about zebras and forget elephants?"

I smiled at her reiteration of the big bull's question and assured her that I would not forget the elephants; I would return to hear their stories.

She urged me to remember my promise, then raised her trunk, opened her mouth, reached inside, and removed a foot-long branch. "Please take this memento so you will think of us." She purposefully laid the limb on the ground and crossed the road to join her family.

Ben and Godfrey's amazement was evident. Clearly they had never seen an adult elephant take anything out of its mouth. While the elephants waited on the far side of the track, I retrieved the mangled branch, whose thorns and leaves had been stripped by the elephant's molars. I promised to return and put the branch in my mouth.

The elephants, satisfied with my pledge, turned and slowly shuffled away. The one who had given me the gift had a stiff left leg that caused her to limp. Godfrey surmised that she had been caught in a small animal snare, which sometimes snagged elephants. He thought that the injury would heal.

Less than a mile from camp, I sadly thought that I had seen my last zebra the previous day. But, after we crested a small rise, by the edge of the path, stood several zebras in the shade of a tree. Godfrey stopped the vehicle and turned off the engine. I immediately locked eyes with the closest zebra, sent our love, and told her that we only wished to take photographs.

"You only want to take our pictures? You don't want to talk?" she asked.

I laughed aloud; her words had refocused me. With my video camera recording, I inquired about the health of her family. She answered that her family was fine and asked if I was the human who had spoken with the zebras that had lost their leader.

I said yes, and asked how she knew.

She answered that there were very few zebras in the area at present, and that her band had been in contact with most of them. She mourned the family's loss and wondered whether the family would stay together. She asked if I had communed with any elephants. I smiled, held up the chewed branch, and asked whether she had spoken to the gifting pachyderm. She said she had, and urged me to keep my promise, because elephants never forget. I assured her that I would keep my word. I asked her name.

She said that zebras didn't have names that humans would recognize, but that she was the family's leader. The head stallion, slightly taller than the mare, stepped forward. His white stripes were tinted orange from a recent dust bath. He lovingly laid his head across her flank.

Godfrey asked her aloud how many were in her family.

She replied, "Eight." When I relayed this information to the group, Ben responded that he only counted five. Much later, after we had reluctantly departed, we encountered the other three members of the family sharing the shade of a tree.

Fiona asked me to ask the zebra how old she was. The zebra heard Fiona's question and did not need me to relay it. She answered, "I am the eldest female in the band, but we do not keep track of age by years."

Fiona asked me how many times the zebra had been pregnant. Again the zebra answered the question immediately. "Four times," and beckoned with her head. Two smaller zebras approached. She introduced them as her daughters and added, "My third child was only one day old when he was killed by hyenas. Also, I've had a miscarriage."

I told her I was sorry and asked about the other members of her family. She said there were three other females, three children, and the stallion.

"Why do equines usually have one male and several females in a band?"

"That is how we perpetuate our species. If we limited ourselves to one male and one female, we would lose even more babies and could not reproduce often enough to survive."

"How long will your children stay with the band?"

"When my daughter is ready to start her own family, she will develop a special scent. Mature males come forward one by one, and her father will conduct interviews in which he psychologically and physically challenges the hopeful suitors. He wants to ensure that the selected stallion is strong and will vigorously defend our daughter, especially during childbirth."

"What does he do at that time?"

"When a female gives birth, she is very vulnerable. The stallion must patrol the area to ensure there are no predators. In unsafe situations, a mare may delay giving birth for nearly a day. After the birth, the father keeps the other zebras at a safe distance, because during the first few minutes of life, it is imperative that the newborn sees only its mother. Her unique striping pattern thus becomes etched in the baby's mind. Sight recognition is most important to us."

"How does a stallion start a family?"

"The father-son relationship is very strong. A male zebra stays with his band as long as he chooses. When he decides to start his own family, he joins a band of bachelors to complete his education. When we are in herds, and hyenas or wild dogs attack, the families are joined by bachelor bands to defend the young. Being social animals, we depend heavily on family and friends. A zebra living alone in the wild is soon dead. We do everything together in the open; eat, play, mate, and sleep. Childbirth is the only time we need privacy."

"Did wild horses live the same way?"

"Yes. For millions of years they lived as we live today. But that changed long ago when horses decided on domestication."

"Did zebras ever try domestication?"

"Yes, along with our close cousins the Quagga, we tried the way of the horse. But it didn't work out. Since the friendly Quagga were quickly shot into extinction, we chose to remain wild.

"Man has decimated zebras like no other predator. Millions of years ago, your ancestors evolved from primates. They lived in trees and used all four limbs to climb and grasp branches. They were originally vegetarians and were prey animals, just like we are. They posed no threat to us at all; we drank side by side for countless generations.

"As the climate became more arid, forests slowly shrank, and food became increasingly scarce for the primates. Gradually, they became omnivores by using their forelimbs as hands to gather grubs, ants, and other insects.

"As forests receded, some ape-like humans descended from the trees and lived part-time on the ground. They became scavenger-gathers, but were often still preyed upon. As early humans learned to use their hands to deftly hold and manipulate objects, they also learned to balance, stand, and run on two legs. Standing upright enabled them to see further and keep predators at a greater distance.

"Your ancestors learned to use sticks, stones, and bones as weapons and to hunt in packs. As time passed, we began to regard humans as predators."

"Why did horses choose domestication?"

"Horses should tell you that story. We chose to remain wild and avoid humans. Because men have since killed millions of zebras, we wonder if we made the right choice. Only relatively few of us are left now, and to continue our way of life, we have to depend on people, because although we are still wild, we are not truly free."

"I don't understand."

"There are few places of safety left for us, and fences further restrict our grazing grounds. What are we to do?"

I explained the zebra's plight to Godfrey. He agreed and sympathized, but was hopeful, because plans were being developed to establish a Transfrontier Conservation Area (TFCA). This agreement would link the game reserves and national parks of many countries, so that wildlife could roam larger areas and have secure migration corridors.

The zebra said that would be a welcome change and hoped it would not be too late.

Since Fiona had to leave, I reluctantly said goodbye to the zebra, who shook her head no and stomped the ground for us to stay. The mare reminded me not to forget the elephants, because their situation was even more desperate than that of the zebras.

We lingered a few more minutes to admire them. The lead mare had barely moved or broken eye contact with me the entire time we had talked. I asked her where horses had decided on domestication.

"There is a place where thousands of equines were hunted and slaughtered long ago. That is where horses chose between remaining wild and facing possible extinction—like zebras do today—or attempting domestication."

Godfrey urged me to conclude my meeting. I thanked the zebra. We drove close to the band as we departed, but they did not flinch. Although I regretted leaving Mashatu, I knew that I would keep my promise and return to write the elephants' story.

"To be loved by a horse, or by any animal,

should fill us with awe — for we have not deserved it."

- Marion C. Garretty

CONSIDERING DOMESTICATION

Lovely and Suny; Solutré, France

I discovered a nineteenth-century drawing by Emile Bayard that depicted primitive men driving horses off a cliff called the Roche de Solutré, near the town of Solutré in central France. Just a mile from the base of the cliff, archeologists had uncovered the bones of more than one hundred thousand horses.

I flew to Lyon, France, rented a car, and drove north along the Saône River under a cloudless sky. The French countryside opened into flat farmland, the Alps appeared on the eastern horizon, and the western foothills of the Massif Central Mountains rimmed the fertile valley.

Vineyards covered the rolling foothills around Macon. A sign welcomed me to Pouilly Fuissé, the heart of France's wine country. North of the equator, the seasons were opposite: instead of spring, it was fall. Golden, orange, and red grapevine leaves vibrantly colored the landscape.

The road to Solutré wound uphill through a patchwork of vineyards. Imposing Mont Pouilly rose from the southern side of the valley; the opposing ridge ended abruptly at the Roche de Solutré.

I tried to visualize the area before human development; no vineyards, towns, or roads, just vast, sweeping valleys filled with grass and rimmed by forested mountains yielding to rocky, snow-covered peaks.

Less than fifty homes, a few shops, and an inn comprised the village of Solutré, situated in the middle of the valley near the base of the cliff. A cluster of thousand-year-old stone buildings encircled the church and its tall clock tower.

A museum, carved into the bottom of the Roche de Solutré like a grotto, was closed until later, so I hiked a well-worn path for an eagle's view of the valley. Adjacent to the cliff, near the town, was the fenced-off archeological site. Blue tarps protected the horses' bones. Vineyards surrounded the town and blanketed the countryside like a giant, multicolored quilt. Further up the valley, they yielded to large grassy fields and small forests. Down the valley and across the Saône River loomed Mont Blanc, the tallest mountain in Europe.

By the time I returned to the parking area, the museum had opened. The exhibits depicted the history of the area and the evolution of human hunting. I struggled to communicate with the sole employee and asked whether anyone in town spoke English. He understood and wrote on a piece of paper, Patrick, Le Pichet de Solutré.

In a small market, I purchased several pounds of carrots and showed the shopkeeper the paper. He smiled and pointed to the inn next door. The quaint pensión had a bar and restaurant. Postcards from around the world papered the walls.

A man with a broad friendly smile appeared and said, "Bonjour, monsieur." I returned his greeting in French. Recognizing my foreign accent, he welcomed me again in my native tongue. I handed him the note; he introduced himself as Patrick. He proudly added that he was the only person in Solutré who spoke English.

After I told Patrick my purpose, he said he owned two horses that I might want to meet. Suny was a gelding acquired shortly after Patrick, and his wife, Nicole, had moved to town. Lovely, bought as a companion for Suny, was an Appaloosa from Colorado. The two horses lived in a pasture overlooking Solutré. He drew a map to the horses' home and said that I was welcome to go there any time.

Early the next morning, after a light rain, sunshine broke through the clouds. The gate to the horses' large field of tall grass was at the base of a slope. The air was fresh; a bright rainbow arched over the infamous cliff.

A whinny of welcome from behind a cluster of bushes preceded the emergence of the two horses. Suny, in the lead, was the taller of the two and had a beautiful chestnut coat with matching mane and tail. He had a wide white blaze, which tapered to a point above his nostrils, and a nose that was rosy pink. Lovely followed closely behind. Her coat was white and lightly dappled with small black spots. She had dark patches on her legs, her belly, and the tip of her nose. Both horses looked radiantly healthy.

I broke a carrot in half. The horses' ears perked, and their pace quickened. I partially turned my back to the horses to present a nonthreatening posture. They walked right up to me to receive their treats.

Suny was first. He smelled me and lightly nudged my back with his nose as a gesture of greeting. I gave him a carrot, which he took gingerly. Lovely circled around to face me, shook her head, and asked for a carrot. I gladly complied and introduced myself as a friend of Patrick and Nicole.

Lovely asked if I liked the rainbow. I told her that it was lovely, like her name. She nickered in laughter and wanted to know where I was from.

When I told her Colorado, she snorted happily and asked why I was in France. I stated my mission and asked if Solutré was a significant place for horses.

"Indeed it is," Suny responded. The horses pranced and asked me to follow them up the hill. The impressive view included the Roche de Solutré, which guarded the far side of the vineyard-filled valley.

I sat on a plastic bag from my pack. Lovely ran her soft nose over my head. Her breath warmed my neck; her whiskers tickled. The two horses touched noses and exchanged whispers. Then Suny blew air on me and ran his muzzle across my shoulders. I relished the horses' attention. We were silent for several minutes, enjoying the sweeping panorama. Finally, I asked them about the horses' decision for domestication.

Suny said, "For millions of years, wild horses, sometimes in large herds, had roamed free across much of the Earth in search of fresh food and clean water. We slowly spread from North America—across the Bering land bridge that connected Alaska to Russia—to Asia, Europe, and Africa. Many migratory, herding herbivores had summer and winter homes, but none moved as fast as the horse. We migrated great distances and had seen most of the world before your human ancestors, living in Africa, first stood upright."

"What did horses look like back then?"

"The local environment usually determined that. Here, they were no taller than a pony, but were thick around the neck, chest, and legs. They had large heads and muscular jaws with hard teeth that could grind the dry, coarse winter grass. The equines were mostly a sandy dun color that matched the surrounding terrain; their manes stood upright. The big, dappled forest horses had large hooves that enabled them to tromp through swamps. In the northern tundra, horses had thick, white coats.

"To the south, equines were small, slim, and swift. They had light tan coats that deflected the sun's strong rays. Near the hot deserts of North Africa and the Near East lived the small onagers and asses that had sandy dun backs and white bellies. Their heads were small; their ears were large and long. Further south, zebras occupied Africa. Equines roamed the world."

"You certainly live in a pretty place."

"Yes, this land once was wonderful for wild horses. In the winter, our ancestors grazed on the floodplain since water was easily accessible, and the snows were never too deep to forage the grass beneath. In the spring, we migrated to the mountains where new grass grew, and water from melting snow was plentiful. Also, moving to higher elevations helped us escape the summer heat and bothersome insects."

"What happened here?"

"Almost half a million years ago, horses encountered the first humans wandering through the land. They were short of stature compared to present-day people. What most intrigued the horses was that humans had learned to control fire and kept them burning throughout the long cold winters. Horses discovered that when they stayed near the human camps that had fire, predators were kept at bay."

"Is that when people started to hunt horses?"

"Humans were still a prey animal, but they were omnivorous. When they could, they scavenged meat from predators. Then another type of human, one you call Neanderthal, moved into the area. They were also short, but thicker than the others. The Neanderthals brought tools; long, pointed wooden stakes, short, thick branches or bones that were used as clubs, and small stones for hurling.

"Over tens of thousands of years, Neanderthals primarily gathered and scavenged their food, but gradually they learned, by imitating wolves, to hunt in packs. The first mammals they killed were small rodents, foxes, and hares. Later, they learned to hunt larger game such as boar and deer. Neanderthals were the first upright walkers to kill a horse. That ill-fated equine had been seriously injured in a fall and could not keep up with her family. Men stabbed and clubbed the injured horse to death.

"People began to hunt healthy horses by working in groups. Most of the time they were unsuccessful, but sometimes they managed to make a kill. They used every part of the animal—even long leg bones would be broken apart to obtain the meaty marrow. One kill gave them hundreds of pounds of meat that could feed a group for a week or more. They removed the hide with sharpened stones and used the skin for protection from the elements.

"This practice continued for thousands of years and instilled the fear of man in us. We came to regard the Neanderthals as predators and decided to live further away from them. That was a major adjustment in our thinking, since earlier in history, when we were both prey animals, horses and humans had drunk from rivers side by side."

"When and how did humans start to hunt horses here?"

"More than thirty thousand years ago, during our migration up the valley, Neanderthals chased a band of horses toward the rocks," said Suny.

"I saw a picture of cavemen forcing horses off the cliff. Did that really happen?"

"No. Humans never made us leap off Solutré. We could run faster and outmaneuver people in an open field.

"When escaping predators, the lead female, who possessed the most knowledge of the area, led the family away from danger in single file. This strategy made it easier to keep track of everyone, and each horse protected the back of the horse in front. A single-file line also made it more difficult for a predator to attack the weakest individual. The lead stallion, usually the biggest and strongest horse in the family, brought up the rear to fend off dangerous pursuers. Zebras still practice this strategy."

"Did bachelor bands use the same tactic?"

"Yes, but bachelor bands have fewer members and are not as close-knit. If a horse were separated, it could become trapped in a natural corral among the rocks, like the one near the bottom of the cliff. Men waiting there would club, stab, and stone the horse to death."

"Did Neanderthals slay all those horses at Solutré?"

"Their small groups usually killed only one horse at a time. Within two or three thousand years, a different kind of human, the one you call Cro-Magnon, came into the area and drove the Neanderthals away. The taller, leaner Cro-Magnon lived in larger groups. Cro-Magnon, or Homo sapiens, was you, modern man.

"They, too, had mastered fire and had learned to attach an antler point to a long thin stake to create a deadly lance that could be thrown. Progressively, the spear's killing power improved as stones, chipped into razor-sharp points, were affixed to the end of a stake. The modern humans with superior weapons outhunted the Neanderthals and often beat them to a kill.

"For the next ten thousand years, during migrations, people still only hunted and killed one or two horses at a time. Losses were similar to those of zebras crossing a crocodile-infested river; a few would be taken, but most crossed safely.

"Did modern man hunt other animals?"

"Humans hunted nearly every type of animal—even the enormous mammoth. Sometimes equines shared this area with reindeer, which humans also hunted. Then, less than twenty thousand years ago, several big changes occurred. The first was communal hunting, which brought separate family groups together.

"Working as a large team, people developed complex hunting strategies. They piled stones to partially block the valley creating a drive lane. Then they hid among the rock piles. Horses almost always choose the path of least resistance, preferring to run around, rather than jump, an obstacle. When a band of horses came grazing up the valley, humans tried to drive them into the natural corral. The results were terrifying: people were able to kill several horses—sometimes even the lead mare or stallion, which destroyed the family unit.

"For the first time in their evolution, people shifted from subsistence living, in which men were primarily involved in hunting and women in gathering fruit, nuts, and roots daily, to surplus living, in which humans hunted seasonally and stored surplus food—enough for everyone for several weeks or months. Not having to hunt every day created time for people to specialize and perfect techniques in making more deadly weapons, including the spear thrower, and invent new tools, like sewing needles."

"What is a spear thrower?"

"It was a straight piece of antler more than two feet long with a notch at one end and a handle at the other. Men would hold onto one end and fit a short, thin spear, tipped with a small, sharpened stone, into the notch. The device doubled the human arm's length and propelled the small spear more than twice the distance a person could throw it.

"Learning from watching birds in flight, people collected feathers and attached them to the end of the spear. This technique made the spear spin, fly more accurately, and hit with greater force. The spear thrower, along with communal hunting, almost guaranteed that several horses would be slaughtered in each hunt, and sometimes an entire family would be wiped out. Our numbers drastically decreased as the human population grew. Communal hunting led to trade. When different families hunted together, they shared their new inventions and weapons, which spread their knowledge.

"But something even more important happened as a result of becoming proficient hunters and having more meat than could be eaten before it spoiled. People began leaving some of the horses' remains behind, which provided easy meals for wolves and other predators. Wolves started living just beyond human encampments. They even followed people on horse hunts. People came to recognize the wolves' warning call and used them as sentries. At some point, a wolf pup was brought into a human's camp and became a close companion. Observing two different predators come together, eat horses, and live side by side, frightened horses immensely."

"What did they do?"

"Horses had always been able to adapt to new surroundings, but never had encountered anything like modern man. More than ten thousand years ago, people started to live year-round in the valley. That was when we first considered domestication. But it would be several thousand years before we found the right circumstances in which to approach people.

"Most large mammals, including humans, had been nomadic, until man started using natural rock walls and the mouths of caves to create semi-permanent camps, which cut off many animals' migratory routes. As the last ice age ended and warm, wet weather followed, the mountain forests spread onto the open grasslands. Throughout most of Western Europe, horse herds were shrinking dramatically. Horses thought that the only chance for survival was to further distance themselves from people. Since humans had become horses' most feared predator, avoiding men was more important than finding the best feeding grounds and watering sites. Horses decided, as had mammoths and reindeer, to relocate.

"Some horses tried to evade humans by living in the forested mountains. Those herds became isolated in the winter and eventually died out. Some horses followed the reindeer north along the Rhine River toward colder climates, but the horses could not survive the deep snows.

"Other herds moved east and followed the Danube River, which provided easy access to water. Whenever they encountered enclaves of people, horses pushed further east. Near the Black Sea, the horses came upon a grassy steppe that extended for hundreds of miles to the north and east, on which very little human habitation existed. But living on the plain all year was difficult due to a lack of food for foraging, so during foaling in the spring, horses moved near the forests for access to nutritious grasses.

"During this time, man had devised the bow and arrow, which doubled his killing range. Due to over-hunting by humans, many of the larger mammals, such as the mammoths, mastodons, and the giant eleven-foot-tall elk, became extinct.

"In addition to the development of more sophisticated tools and weaponry, humans began to cultivate wheat and barley. Horses observed that wild goats, sheep, pigs, and oxen had chosen domestication over potential extermination. Although the domesticated animals were protected from predators, they were raised only for their meat, milk, and hides. Plus, domestication restricted the animals' natural behaviors, which did not appeal to horses.

"When people began to use oxen to carry cargo, the ox became highly valued. Horses realized that if they could become valuable to people for something other than meat, they could ensure their survival. Horses decided to try to become a companion to people like the wolf-dog had."

"How did you learn all of this?"

"I was raised in this valley with a herd of horses that told me the history of horses here," answered Suny.

"I learned the story from Suny and hope one day to return to America to recount the tale to other horses. I have been trying to convey my wish to Nicole and Patrick," added Lovely.

"How did horses originally learn to live with people?"

Lovely answered, "Many horses know the inspirational story of Sunshine."

I asked, "Was Sunshine a horse?"

"Sunshine was a girl and the first horse whisperer. She saved a horse's life, gained our trust, and is our hero, as well as the symbol of our hope for humanity."

"Is Sunshine the reason horses like women so much?"

"Yes. All women have some Sunshine in them."

I gave the horses the rest of the carrots, then hugged and thanked my new friends.

At dinner, I related the horses' conversation to Patrick and Nicole, who confided that they were planning to sell the pensión and travel to America. I told them about Lovely's desire to return to Colorado and was relieved to learn that Lovely's original owner would be happy to buy her back. Apparently, Lovely's telepathic message had been heard.

I, too, was eager to return to Colorado, visit Bess, and learn Sunshine's story.

"Horses and children, I often think,

have a lot of the good sense there is in the world."

- JOSEPHINE DEMOTT ROBINSON

SUNSHINE

Sundance; Steamboat Lake, Colorado

After my enlightening journey, I was eager to be home and see Bess. From the top of Rabbit Ears Pass, I watched the Yampa River meander through the wide valley below. The hilly horizon stretched on forever—a perfect home for horses, in which each season paints a different picture. As it was November, the aspens were bare and the grasses brown; only the evergreens brightened the muted landscape. In their shadows, patches of snow lingered from an early storm. The autumn days, when the sunlit aspen leaves glittered gold and the mountains shimmered in the wind, had passed; winter's white blanket loomed.

I fell asleep happily anticipating seeing Bess. The next day was clear and cold. I entered her pasture with an armload of carrots. The horses grazed at the far end of the field. When I called, several looked in my direction, and one slowly sauntered toward me. I thought it was Bess, and then realized that it was her son, whose thick winter coat made him look as large as his mother. I gave him a huge hug.

He nickered a welcome. "It is great to see you, Sundance," I said, while stroking his neck and looking around for Bess.

Sundance softly said, "Mom is not here."

"Is she in another pasture?"

"Bess has gone."

"What do you mean gone? Is she okay? Is she sick? Is she at the vet's?" I asked rapidly without giving Sundance time to reply.

"Bess is okay, but she has gone where we all go one day."

"She died?"

"Yes."

My eyes filled with tears. I dropped the carrots and collapsed to the ground. Sundance brushed a tear from my face. I closed my eyes and sobbed as all that Bess had taught me flashed through my mind. When I opened my eyes, the horses had encircled me. I had lost a close friend and felt paralyzed because I could not thank her.

Reading my mind Sundance said, "You can thank Bess anytime."

"Can Bess hear me?"

"It comforts me to talk to her."

I thanked Bess and sent a silent prayer.

Sundance stood beside me and waited for me to finish, then asked, "Are those carrots for us?"

I smiled, gave out the treats, and asked if she passed peacefully.

"Bess died in her sleep," answered Cash.

"How young was she?"

"Bess was twenty-six. She was my pair-bond mate and my best friend."

"I'm sorry, Cash."

"We're lucky to be well cared for. But now we have an odd number of horses, and I feel left out."

"Cash, I will talk to the owners about that. When did Bess pass?"

"When the aspen leaves were gold, her favorite time of year."

I sighed deeply. "Mine too," was all I could muster. Looking down, I spied a perfect golden leaf. I pressed it into my notebook in remembrance.

"Where have you been?" asked Sundance.

His words brought me back to the present, so I recounted my adventures.

"You talked with our cousins in striped pajamas?" asked Dainty excitedly.

"Yes, the zebras were amazing."

The horses were pleased with my efforts. I mentioned the story of Sunshine. Nodding, Sundance said that that was the tale he had wanted to tell when we first met. As evening approached, Sundance asked me to return in the morning when he would relate Sunshine's saga.

The next day was warmer. I brought more baby carrots and good news: I had spoken to their human companions, and they had promised to maintain an even number of horses in the field. Several equines nickered in appreciation. After the horses had snacked on their treats, I asked Sundance about Sunshine.

"My mom told me the tale many times. Sunshine lived about ten thousand years ago, not far from the Black Sea. Her people had come from the south and dwelled in low-lying hills near the grassy steppe. She lived with her parents and an older sister. They were one of several families in a large band of humans. The clan had built mud-thatched huts in a circle near a south-facing rock wall. Inside the circle was a corral for domestic sheep.

"Our ancestors observed Sunshine's people cultivating wheat. Watching humans purposefully working the land was gratifying. Horses have always cultivated the earth by spreading seeds. Equines only assimilate part of our food; the rest passes through us whole and is often expelled miles from where it was consumed. Plus, while we walk, our hooves loosen and aerate the soil to help the seeds germinate. We hoped that humans growing wheat might lead to a new dialogue with people."

"What do you mean?"

"Horses can converse in several ways: body position, miniscule movement, resonating, in which we sense the same thing, and telepathy. Plus, we understand the symbolism of flowers."

"Flowers have different meanings?"

"Yes, each species has a message that is known by many animals, although people have forgotten most of the flowers' meanings."

"In Africa, an elephant gave me an acacia branch. What does it mean?"

"Did the acacia have its leaves and thorns when you received it?"

"They had been chewed off."

"The acacia symbolizes friendship from the giver. Stripped of leaves and thorns, it implies hope in the face of adversity."

"Wow! What are some other flowers' meanings?"

"What do you think the olive blossom stands for?"

"Peace," popped into my mind.

"Correct. And what does a rose represent?"

"Love," I answered without thinking.

"See, you know some of the flowers' language."

"What did the cultivation of wheat mean to the horses?"

"The wheat stalk represents riches, which meant that humans had learned to harvest wealth from the earth. It was a significant sign—the horses wanted to get to know those people better."

"How did that happen?"

"For several seasons, a band of horses cautiously observed Sunshine's clan from afar. One sunny spring day, after weeks of continuous rain, the horses appeared to the people during their celebration of a birth.

"Sunshine later told the horses that it was she who was ceremoniously presented to the sky and named in honor of the shining sun. The appearance of horses for the first time in anyone's memory was a good omen. Previously, Sunshine's people knew of horses only through stories and by an amulet kept by the shaman.

"After the ceremony, a group of humans pursued the horses, who withdrew into the trees. The people followed the steeds until their tracks disappeared into a large river.

"Horses continued to observe the community of wheat growers but did not show themselves again for several years. Herds lived most of the year on the vast steppe, a sometimes difficult environment in which to flourish.

"Sunshine said that the horses' appearance had made the clan's shaman optimistic about the future. He possessed many tiny animal figurines, passed down for generations, for use in the children's rite of passage into adulthood. The small carvings included several different birds, fish, otter, fox, hare, deer, sheep, goat, auroch, and a horse.

"By the age of eight, children had learned to perform many tasks that benefited the community. When a child turned ten, the shaman chose a specific animal figurine for the youth. The child would spend six moon cycles learning as much as possible about that animal: where it lived, what food it ate, when it slept, how it gave birth and raised its young, and how the animal interacted with its environment. At the end of the period, the child would meet with the clan's leaders and share what he or she had learned, as well as describe the effects of those experiences on the youth.

"If the elders were not satisfied, a different animal was assigned to the young person to study for the next six moons. But if lessons had been learned well, the youth would be allowed to carve a figurine of that animal to keep. In this way, every generation had expert, intimate, firsthand knowledge of an aspect in their surroundings, a skill that generalized into living in the moment by attending to every small detail of an environment. Since the shaman had never actually seen a horse, he had never selected the equine figurine for anyone.

"The horses began to roam through the area near the people every spring, because the grass was more nutritious there than on the steppe. When the horses showed themselves for the second time, Sunshine's mother was digging roots while her daughter played with a handful of wheat. When Sunshine wandered to the middle of the field, the lead mare emerged from the trees. The rest of the horses remained hidden. The mare slowly approached the young girl until she towered over Sunshine, who stood completely still. Then, without any fear, she offered the wheat to the horse.

"Sunshine's mother glanced up as the mare took a mouthful of wheat. Stunned by the sight of the horse, she couldn't move or speak for several moments. She watched in mute fear as Sunshine stood on her tiptoes, and the mare lowered her head, until their lips touched. This made the child laugh, the horse whinny, and the mother gasp, which startled the mare, who quickly retreated into the forest.

"The story of Sunshine's interaction with the horse was often retold. The band was spotted every year thereafter in the early spring. Each time, the horses were seen only from afar, and only when Sunshine was present. Some people wanted to hunt them. This led to a meeting among the elders, who wanted to know more about horses. As this was Sunshine's tenth year, the shaman decided to give the equine carving to her. Sunshine was honored, because in living memory, it had never been given to anyone.

"After receiving the amulet, every day for a full moon cycle, Sunshine returned to the field in which she had met the mare. She left her hut before sunrise with an armful of wheat. She spread the wheat as a gift for the horses, waited for hours by the far edge of the field, then returned to the settlement at dusk.

"One morning, just before the second full moon of her rite of passage, Sunshine sat patiently in the field, when a band of horses, led by a large mare, came into the open to graze. Sunshine remained motionless while delightedly watching the horses feast on the wheat.

"The horses looked like a family to her, because they moved in a tight-knit group. The adults had muscular chests and legs. All had matching reddish brown coats with black, bristly, upright manes and brown-striped legs. The younger horses were leaner. Sunshine noticed that the horses had unusual feet, because their track was like no other animal she had ever seen. It looked like an upside down cup.

"In the horses' presence, Sunshine remained still and did not try to approach. Over several weeks, she observed that the horses almost always moved in the same order and were led by the tall mare, the largest horse in the family except for the stallion, who stayed behind the band to keep a sharp lookout. The lead mare was followed by her two daughters, a second adult female, her two sons, a third mature mare, a little filly, and finally, the smallest adult mare. Three of the four adult females had large bellies and looked pregnant.

"Sunshine relished watching the horses eat, run, groom each other, and roll in the dirt. She especially loved observing the young horses play.

"Sunshine noticed that when alarmed, the horses sent silent signals to the others who immediately stopped, held their heads high, and perked their ears. They motionlessly awaited a signal. In potentially dangerous situations, the lead mare would immediately steer the group away from the threat. All the horses followed in order; the stallion came last. At such times, Sunshine climbed as high into a tree as she could for safety.

"As the days passed, Sunshine learned the horses' body language. A lowered head indicated curiosity, or submission, except when the stallion used that action in conjunction with baring his teeth to direct the horses. Pinned-back ears meant displeasure. A horse pointing both ears in one direction signified alertness.

"The horses slowly became comfortable in Sunshine's presence and began to graze and play increasingly closer to her. During the third cycle of the moon, Sunshine thought she heard the lead mare say, 'We can be friends,' but had heard no utterance: the communication felt as though the mare had spoken inside Sunshine's mind. Sunshine was puzzled, until she shared her experience with her older sister and friends. Some said that they too had had unusual experiences of silent speaking with their special animals.

"Sunshine repeatedly heard the statement 'We can be friends' from the lead mare. Eventually, she replied silently, 'I would like that.' A query from the mare entered Sunshine's mind: would she walk with the horses through the trees into the next field away from the human hunters?

"Sunshine looked around but could see no people. The mare explained that the horses could sense the hidden hunters. The family had become accustomed to Sunshine's scent, but they were uncertain about the others. Sunshine willingly followed the horses into the woods. The stallion stayed behind to ensure that the family was not followed.

"Sunshine walked in silence through the forest. Before leaving the woods, the mare nipped a strand of ivy from a branch. The horses gathered around the girl as the mare dropped the vine at Sunshine's feet. She was surprised at the gesture, because to her people, ivy signified the offering of friendship.

"The horses then paraded in single file around Sunshine. They relaxed their ears, lowered their heads, showed their tongues, and smacked their lips. Sunshine mimicked the friendly gestures and felt overwhelming joy. This monumental milestone made Sunshine the first person to be befriended by a family of equines.

"In that far field, the horses broke their circle to start grazing, playing, and prancing. The young horses led Sunshine away from the adults to join their running game and purposefully slowed so that she could keep up. The lead mare and stallion groomed one another while keeping a lookout.

"Later, each horse personally greeted Sunshine. That day, for the first time, she touched and stroked each of the horses. They were shedding their winter coats; Sunshine saved several tufts of hair. She even rolled on the ground to take a dust bath. The horses nickered and lightly stamped the ground in amusement. It was the most amazing day of Sunshine's life, and she was reluctant to leave. At sunset, she thanked the horses and promised to return to the distant field the following day.

"By the end of the third full moon of her animal rite of passage, the days warmed and new grass sprouted everywhere. Sunshine spent those delightful days walking, running, and sitting with her equine friends. She watched the pregnant mares' bellies bulge as their foaling times neared.

"Early one morning, the stallion signaled that it was safe for the lead mare to lie down in the high grass to give birth. The stallion continually circled the field looking for predators and kept his family and Sunshine at a distance from the foaling mare, so Sunshine was unable to actually witness the birth.

"Finally, the mare rose, and some minutes later, with her mother's encouragement, the tiny, defenseless baby staggered to its feet, stumbled, and fell. After several attempts at standing, the struggling foal's legs steadied, and she took her first wobbly steps. The new mother licked her baby dry then directed her with a nudge and a soft whinny to her milk-filled teats. She shielded the filly from the others during this bonding period, so that the foal would imprint her mother's image in her mind.

"Later, the foal's sisters joined the pair and took turns nuzzling the baby. As soon as the filly had a steady walk, the stallion signaled the family. The lead mare took the group through some trees, across a creek, and into a fresh field. There, the family could graze safely away from the scent of the birth.

"The whole family was energized. During the afternoon, each became acquainted with the new addition. The lead mare then introduced her foal to Sunshine, who imitated the nuzzling gestures of the horses. From the day she was born, the foal trusted Sunshine as a member of the family.

"Several days later, Sunshine was privileged to attend the second mare's birth. Again the stallion circled the chosen field to check the area and herded the other horses away. The expectant mother circled the field several times. On one pass, Sunshine saw two tiny hooves enclosed in a membrane protruding from the back of the mare. Sunshine climbed a nearby tree to watch. A few minutes later, the mare rolled onto her back and pushed hard. The two legs inched out with the head tucked tightly between them. The sack broke, and liquid gushed out. The mare repeatedly pushed, and the baby slowly began to emerge. The mare paused, gathered her strength, and made a powerful push; the filly slipped out.

"The mare remained on the ground and began to lick her newborn baby. After the foal was clean and dry, she tenuously rose to her feet, swaying back and forth. She was having her first meal when the stallion gave an alarm call. He had caught the scent of predators and wanted to guide his family to safety. Sunshine, still safely in the tree, saw one, then several, wolves fan out across the field.

"The stallion guided his family into the woods and returned to prod the new mother and her stumbling filly to safety. As the wolves moved in, the mare and the stallion tried to protect the baby. One of the stallion's kicks sent a wolf flying in screaming pain, but the rest tightened their circle. One wolf crept behind the horses. While the others distracted the adults, the lone wolf grabbed the foal's leg and dragged her to the ground. The other wolves rushed in, and she disappeared under their bodies. The parents tried to rescue the foal, but they were finally forced to abandon the baby. The family retreated into the forest. Sunshine watched in horror as the filly was quickly devoured. She cried long into the night.

"Sunshine did not see the horses again until after the fourth full moon. She sadly wandered through many meadows in search of her friends. One day, she sat sobbing in a field close to her home when she heard a whinny of welcome. A horse at the far edge of the field beckoned to her, then disappeared into the shadows.

"Excitedly, Sunshine followed the mare through the trees to where the rest of the band grazed, sat on the ground, and waited for the horses to approach her. There was a new foal, whose long legs and huge head looked too big for her small body. Sunshine greeted each horse and was astonished at how much the lead mare's baby had grown.

"The lengthening summer days were wonderful for Sunshine as she walked, ran, and played with the horses. One day, the horses' meanderings led Sunshine further from her people than she had ever been, so when evening approached, the horses accompanied her home.

"The next morning, Sunshine could not locate the family. She followed the freshest tracks through fields and groves of trees. She was elated to discover them at the edge of a meadow. But something was wrong. As Sunshine approached, she noticed that the horses were huddled together and anxious. The lead mare's foal lay on the ground whinnying in pain.

"Sunshine looked carefully at the injured baby. The lead mare was gently licking a small wound on her foal's lower leg to clean it, as well as to prevent the scent of blood from escaping into the air. The mare looked at Sunshine, shook her head, and pawed the ground with her hoof. Sunshine clearly heard her plea for help. The horses knew that if the injured baby could not keep up with the family, she would quickly fall victim to predators.

"The mother tried to pacify her daughter by licking her face and talking to her soothingly. Sunshine edged nearer to the small horse and spoke to her in a calm, reassuring manner. Sunshine examined the wound and felt a long, thin ridge beneath the baby's skin. She determined it to be a splinter and remembered watching her father remove a sliver from her sister's foot.

"Sunshine explained what she would do. While the lead mare continued to lick the baby's face to keep her still, Sunshine gently opened the cut as she pushed the sliver towards the entry wound until a piece of wood protruded. She pinched the wood between her fingernails and pulled. In one smooth stroke, the long splinter was out, and the little horse sighed in relief.

"The lead mare neighed triumphantly and encouraged her baby to stand. The small filly rose to her feet and moved with no pain. She licked Sunshine's face repeatedly making Sunshine giggle.

"Suddenly, sensing danger, several horses stopped grazing. The stallion signaled, and the family rapidly retreated. Sunshine started to run. With only two legs to propel her, she fell behind and froze when she heard a wolf howl. Several wolves echoed to signal their positions. Frightened, Sunshine ran toward the nearest tree, yelling loudly to frighten the wolves. Momentarily, they paused.

"The horses, already a safe distance away, heard Sunshine's screams. The lead mare started to double back but was blocked by the stallion. She dodged her mate and galloped full speed toward Sunshine. The stallion directed the rest of his family further away from the wolves. He knew that the wolves were not a threat to a healthy adult horse, but his foals were at risk.

"Sunshine saw several pairs of ears shifting in the tall grass as the wolves encircled her. Suddenly, she heard pounding hooves. A few seconds later, the lead mare was by her side. Although she knew that she could not protect Sunshine for very long, the mare boldly confronted the wolves. Confused by the presence of the big horse, the wolves froze in place.

"Then, without hesitation, the mare laid down and rolled onto her side so that her belly faced the wolves. At first, Sunshine thought that the mare was sacrificing herself to save her. She pushed on the mare's back to make her stand. The mare stretched her long neck around Sunshine, held her firmly, and in one surge of motion, rolled onto her stomach and rose to her feet. Draped over the mare's back, Sunshine clutched the horse's upright mane and swung a leg over the mare's side. Straddling the horse's back, she squeezed her legs tightly. The mare bolted.

"The wolves pursued the fleeing pair. One wolf tried to bite the mare's rear leg, but she kicked back and knocked the yelping wolf away. The mare lengthened her stride. She ran so fast that Sunshine had tears in her eyes. After a few moments, the confused wolves gave up the chase.

"The mare slowed when she reached the other horses. Sunshine loosened her grip and sat upright. She felt tall on the back of the horse. After she slipped off the mare, the horses happily huddled around them.

"Sunshine could not believe how the mare had saved her life and how far and fast they had traveled in such a short time. Sunshine hugged and thanked her. The mare wrapped her neck around Sunshine to return her thanks."

"Sunshine was the first person to ride a horse?"

"Yes. That's when horses' appreciation for the female of your species began. Sunshine had patience and learned our language. When we began to trust her, she was kind to us. She was never aggressive. She accepted us as we were and shared her food. She never tried to control us; she simply wished to know us as fellow beings. Sunshine represents what we admire most in humans; kindness, patience, understanding, compassion, generosity, and most importantly, love."

"What happened next?"

"Sunshine was now more than a friend; she had become part of the band. The lead mare invited her on a journey. Sunshine was thrilled with the idea, but said she would have to ask the village elders.

"That evening Sunshine recounted her adventure. Many people thought the story was too fantastic to be true. She wanted to prove to them that her relationship with the horses was real. Sunshine asked permission to travel with the horses. The adults were skeptical, but since youths had been allowed to stay out overnight during their rites of passage, the elders approved.

"Sunshine was exhilarated. On the fifth full moon, Sunshine's parents packed a satchel of food and accompanied her to the edge of the field where they had first sighted the horses. She kissed and hugged her parents then proceeded into the forest. She was unaware that she was discreetly being followed.

"Half the day passed before Sunshine saw the horses. They appeared tense and did not come forward to welcome her. She greeted and talked to them, and although they meandered into the open, they remained in their arranged order, aware of potential danger. The nervous horses quickened their gait from a slow walk to an amble; Sunshine had to jog to keep pace. The horses told her that people were following them. Sunshine sprinted away; the horses matched her pace. When she stopped to catch her breath, the entire family halted.

"Sunshine hoped they had lost the people, but the horses said that they had not. Then the lead mare lay on her side as she had done when they escaped the wolves. Sunshine understood the mare's intention and swung one leg over her back. She held onto the horse's mane as she stood. The lead mare then galloped away; the family following closely. In the distance, forced from the cover of the trees, four men ran to keep pace. Sunshine smiled as the horses easily outdistanced the men until they were out of sight.

"The mare slowed, the others followed her lead. When they stopped to drink at a stream, Sunshine slipped off the mare's back. She said that her second ride was thrilling, because it was not life threatening, and they had effortlessly lost the pursuing men. She enjoyed the broad perspective horseback riding afforded.

"The lead mare asked Sunshine how much food she had brought. She said she had enough for several days. After ensuring that everyone had had enough to drink, the mare leisurely crossed the creek and headed onto the vast prairie. It was the end of summer; much of the grass had turned brown. The trees behind them disappeared. The stallion silently signaled to the horses to spread out and graze as they walked.

"Since the barren land made it difficult for humans to survive, people usually did not venture onto the steppe. The horses grazed, walked, romped, played, and groomed each other for the remainder of the day. The family continued to trail the mare through the night and into the next day, pausing only when the foals needed to rest.

"Sunshine wondered where they were going. The mare told her to a large gathering near the big water. Sunshine did not understand what she meant but followed the horses trustingly. She asked the lead mare how she knew where the big water was in the boundless field. The mare said that she had been led there by her mother many times and had learned to use her senses.

"The mare explained that horses used their eyes to note the rising and setting of the sun, which guided them in a general direction. Their sensitive ears indicated changing elevation by air pressure. Horses also used their lips and tongue to taste the minerals and moisture content in the soil, which helped establish location, while moisture in the foliage revealed the proximity to water. In traveling great distances, the different regions' plants and animals—especially birds—helped identify the locale. When nearing the big water, horses could smell it.

"The horses trekked through a second moonlit night. When the sky started to lighten on the third day, they were still walking toward the rising sun. By full daylight, the big water, extending beyond the horizon, lay before the family. In the half-light of the previous night, Sunshine had thought the sea was still the vast grassy plain; she had never realized so much water existed in one place. She had seen streams, rivers, and lakes, but nothing like the Black Sea.

"Sunshine asked the mare where all the water came from. The horse told her that many rivers flowed into the sea. Sunshine asked where the rivers got their water. The mare said that the water came from rain and melting snow. Sunshine noted that it snowed a little in the settlement, but that the snow was gone by the beginning of spring, after which the brooks and streams gradually dried up, but the river by the settlement flowed year-round. She wondered why. The mare said that there were places, especially in the massive mountains, where the snow was very deep and never completely melted. Sunshine had heard stories about the big mountains from the clan's elders.

"The mare led the family to the edge of the sea. While they walked, some of the horses nibbled the leaves of small plants that had delicate white flowers. Sunshine had never seen them and picked several to bring back to her clan.

"She followed the family to the pebbly beach where the horses groomed each other and played. Several horses galloped into the water, spraying it with their long legs. Sunshine followed them. The cool water felt good on her skin. She drank some, but quickly spit out the strange-tasting salty water. She repeated her performance to the great amusement of the horses.

"Keeping the big water to their right, the family headed north. Late in the afternoon, the stallion stopped abruptly and sent an alarm by silently shaking his head. The family lined up and trotted away from the sea. Sunshine wondered what was wrong. The stallion said that the smell of blood was in the air. Since a predator might be lurking near the water, he preferred keeping the family out of sight. The lead mare and stallion considered the strengths and weaknesses of each individual to protect them better. The stallion was being extra cautious, because Sunshine could not run as fast or as far as the horses, and he did not want to lose her or any of his family. Sunshine felt the love that bound the horses together.

"They trekked through the immense plain all night only taking periodic breaks to rest or drink. In the middle of the night, the horses became much more animated. Sunshine could sense their energy as they pranced around her. It was not until daylight that she realized the plain was filled with horses. Numerous families mingled as they grazed. Many looked similar to her band, but some were noticeably different. One family was all sandy brown with large heads supported by thick necks. A few others were taller, dapple-gray in color, and more muscular in the chest and legs.

"The lead mare told Sunshine that the horses gathered from all over the land to socialize before they began their fall migration. When the seasons changed, it was safer to cross wide rivers and move to fresh pastures as a herd. After the journey, the families would separate until they gathered again the following season.

"The family approached the other horses in their prearranged order. The lead mare stopped her group at the outside edge of the gathering and waited. Some horses showed interest in the girl but demonstrated no concern for their safety, since she walked within a family band. The stallion then sprinted into the middle of the herd while the lead mare watched the family. He briefly met with several stallions and signaled with a twist of his head for the mare to lead her family away from the herd.

"Sunshine wanted to stay longer and hoped that she had done nothing wrong. The lead mare assured her that she had not, but since the horses would be migrating soon, the stallion needed time to lead the girl home.

"It took the family two days to reach land that was familiar to Sunshine; it took less than half that time for the horses to return to the herd. Sunshine was very sad to see the horses depart, but they promised to return in the spring.

"When she walked into the village, the people were overjoyed by her safe return. They believed all she told them, because the hunters had reported her ride on the back of a horse.

"On the sixth full moon after the start of her rite of passage, Sunshine met with the elders. She recounted her adventures and the way in which the horses had accepted, helped, and protected her. They were amazed by her accomplishment and her foresight in bringing home plants no one had ever seen. The next year, she led a small party of adults across the steppe to the big water and home again.

"Sunshine matured to become the first woman to lead her community. Every spring, her people welcomed the horses' return by sharing their wheat and never hunting them. The relationship between people and horses thrived during Sunshine's lifetime. The horses thought this was an ideal situation and were extremely happy. Their future was full of hope.

"Unfortunately, tragedy struck this horse-human connection after Sunshine, who had lived a long happy life, passed away. Hunters from the clan killed several horses as a sacrifice for Sunshine. This aggressive action revived the horses' fear of people; the equines retreated from the human encampment into the steppe near the inhospitable desert, and the interspecies relationship regressed for another thousand years. Yet horses have never forgotten Sunshine and still cherish her qualities in people."

"What happened next?"

"That story should be told by working horses," answered Cash. "A friend of mine in the next pasture has a sister named Lolly, who lives on a small working ranch near Melbourne. There, horses and people still work the land the way they did before motorized engines were invented."

"You want me to go to Australia?"

"That would be Bess's wish."

"Give a horse what he needs

and he will give you his heart in return."

- Anonymous

WORK HORSES

Bonnie, Lolly, and Sophie;
Victoria, Australia

The Phillip Island Nature Park is adjacent to Bass Strait, which separates mainland Australia from Tasmania. Churchill Island sits in the calm bay created by its big brother, Phillip Island. At low tide a person can walk between the islands.

In November, the middle of spring in Australia, I crossed a long bridge from the mainland and purchased tickets to The Koala Conservation Centre and Churchill Island's historic farm. A small herd of horned cattle grazed in an open field bounded by the bay. The only modern building on the island contained a check-in area and the park rangers' offices. I asked to meet the person in charge of the horses and was referred to Scott Campbell, an equine expert and manager of the farming operation.

The ticket checker pointed toward several old cabins, and said that Scott would be in one of the barns behind them.

I walked among free-ranging chickens and found Scott lubricating a hay-cutting machine. I introduced myself; he shook hands firmly. At first, his strong, lilting Scottish accent was difficult to understand, even though he had moved from his homeland to work on Churchill Island more than twenty years ago.

Scott introduced me to the farm's three draft horses. Seven-year-old Lolly had come from America, and eight-year-old Sophie had been brought from the Clyde Valley in Lanarkshire, Scotland, where the Clydesdale breed originated. Both were roan-colored with wide white blazes on their faces and long dark manes. Although they had come from different continents, they could have been twins. Both stood more than sixteen hands high, and each weighed over eighteen hundred pounds. Bonnie, the tallest horse, was a Percheron purchased the year before when Sophie was sick. Bonnie had a light dapple-gray coat and weighed more than a ton.

The huge horses were waiting for Scott by the gate of their paddock. He said his friends had very gentle dispositions. I mentioned having carrots. Scott asked me to feed Lolly and Bonnie after they had finished work, but said that Sophie could have some now, because she felt sad about being left behind. He added that all of the horses would rather work together, but the hay cutter was only rigged for two horses. After Scott led the other horses away, I consoled Sophie by giving her some treats, and then rejoined him. He noted that Bonnie was strong enough to pull the hay cutter alone, but the horses liked to work as a team.

We washed and dried the horses after they had finished their chores. Scott showed me one of their old horseshoes, which was as wide as my two feet. He gave both horses a portion of oats and said, "It is far better to drive horses with treats than with a whip."

We led the horses back to their seaside corral. Sophie was anxiously pacing but stopped to whicker a welcome. Scott left me with the steeds while he attended to other tasks.

I asked the horses how they liked living on the farm. The horses said they loved their home and thought Scott was part equine, because he was an exceptional man.

He always treated the horses fairly and never overworked or hurt them. Scott also kept the stables immaculate and dry but rarely kept the horses inside, except in inclement weather. Plus, he gave them sweet treats before and after each workout.

I asked the horses what produce grew on the farm.

Sophie said, "The people plant oats, potatoes, wheat, barley, and hay, and raise cattle, goats, chickens, and peacocks."

Lolly added, "This tiny island was the site of the first European garden and wheat crop in Australia. We are part of the plan to preserve and demonstrate the way of life before engines were invented."

"Can you tell me about the history of equine domestication?" I asked.

Bonnie answered, "Horses had hopefully anticipated living with people as their companions. But not only was freedom taken from the horses, they never imagined implements like bits, spurs, and hobbles being used to make them serve as slaves."

"When did domestication begin?"

"More than eight thousand years ago. The slaughter of horses by humans caused them to retreat far from people. To the south, vast deserts and high mountains separated horses from their brethren—the asses, onagers, and zebras. The growing human population in Europe blocked westward migration, and the north's winters were too inhospitable. So horses traveled east toward North America, where they had originated, but the Bering land bridge had submerged under the rising sea, which forced them to live on the open prairie. Living on the steppe was arduous during winter; food was limited, and at times, the winds made the region one of the coldest places on Earth. But at least, there were no human hunters.

"Then a group of people moved further north into the grassland—the horses' last refuge. They brought with them domesticated cattle and sheep. Some of the cattle were used as pack animals to carry the humans' cargo."

"How did they stay warm in winter?"

"Trees were rare on the plain, so people used dried dung for fuel. Horses observed these people for several years as they slowly drifted further onto the steppe. They telepathically screamed warnings to the people, cattle, and sheep about the harshness of the land and urged them to turn back. The domestic animals understood the horses' message and grew restless as they attempted to relate the danger to the people, but the humans continued to move further onto the boundless plain.

"One exceptionally severe winter, while snowstorms raged across the steppe, the cattle and sheep could not dig through the deep snow with their hooves to reach the grass. The people tried unsuccessfully to clear the land of snow, but all of the livestock slowly starved to death, as did some of the people. The remaining people could not move their supplies without the cattle and had little chance for survival. Although the horses had hoped to help these humans, a connection had not been made.

"Later that spring, just after the mares gave birth, the horses were caught by surprise at a small lake. The people had set a trap. The wind coming from the water had concealed the human scent. Most of the herd was drinking when the people attacked and shot several adults with arrows and snared a few foals with nets. Then the people chased the remaining horses into the water and waited. The exhausted steeds were eventually overcome one by one as they tried to emerge from the lake."

"How were the people able to subdue the horses?"

"The desperate humans had considerable experience controlling cattle. They tied the horses' hooves together to prevent them from kicking or running. The people then planted poles and tied the mares securely to them. The foals were left unbound because they never strayed far from their confined milk-bearing mothers. After the foals had nursed, the starving people milked the immobilized mares and were able to survive. The people handled the foals constantly, so they would get used to human contact. They cut grass to feed the bound horses and gradually loosened the ropes to allow some freedom of movement.

"Over time, many of the adult horses needed fewer restraints. Some had only their front hooves bound and could hop around to graze. However, if they tried to chew their bonds, their muzzles were bound. Other horses lashed out at the men when a rope was removed. Those horses remained tightly tied.

"Gradually, the horses realized that the nursing mares and foals received tender care from the women. Their calm presence helped control resistance. At first, people kept the horses, as they had sheep, for their milk and meat. But the group knew that if they wanted to escape the harsh surroundings and return to the land of trees, they would need the horses' help. So they taught the horses, as they had the cattle, to carry cargo.

"Men initially tried to master the adult horses, but since this was very dangerous, they concentrated on the foals. First, they bound the young equines so they could not reject the unfamiliar weight that was securely strapped to their backs. Slowly, the young horses became accustomed to packs, and eventually, grew into adults that had no fear of people or aversion to cargo.

"On the steppe, horses were easier to care for than cattle. The people survived because of the steeds and returned to the forests, taking with them one of man's most valuable assets: the disciplined horse.

"Other large animals like the camel and oxen had chosen domestication earlier, but neither had proved to be as adaptable as horses. Unfortunately, those equines learned that domestication was synonymous with slavery, yet they lived with the hope of better circumstances. Our ancestors would have to wait many centuries before man realized that horses made great companions as well as fine teachers.

"After generations of domestication, a well-trained horse had equal value to several head of cattle or a small flock of sheep. Word of the horse's usefulness spread from the steppe to the Far East, the Balkans, and Europe. As more people learned the worth of skilled horses, societies were built around us."

"Did people first ride or drive horses?"

"In the beginning, horses followed the same path of domestication as oxen and sheep; kept only for our milk and meat. Many people to this day still consume horsemeat. Then horses learned to carry cargo for humans. Old, young, and infirm people had ridden oxen for ages, which to oxen, was the same as carrying cargo. A nose-ring was invented to control the oxen, but horses resisted the nose-ring and would rip it from their soft flesh, which created a painful, bloody mess. Thus, a rope halter with a nose-band was developed to rein in the horse. The inefficient nose-band restricted the horses' breathing, so people frequently slit horses' nostrils several inches up the nose. Although this painful, disfiguring practice did not work, it was continued for thousands of years.

"After the wheel was invented, horses were strapped to wagons with harnesses that choked them. The harness allowed a horse to use more of its strength, which increased the load a horse could pull by as much as five times. But, for a thousand generations, horses suffered and some suffocated to death, until the padded yoke collar that did not impede their breathing was designed.

"The horses' ability to carry cargo and people faster than any other animal set equines apart. For many generations, a man's wealth was measured by the number of horses he owned. In ancient China, a horse's life was so valuable that sometimes, if a horse doctor's patient died, so did the doctor.

"Then the Roman Empire's thirty thousand miles of stone roads were built to accommodate two or four horses traveling abreast. Carts, chariots, wagons, and even rails for trains were built with wheels a particular distance apart to accommodate horses."

"What was man's worst invention for horses?"

"The bit," the three horses cried in unison.

Sophie continued, "People tried many methods to control horses. One practice was to loop a rope around a horse's lower jaw and jerk it in the direction a man wanted to go. This practice frequently fractured or injured the horse's jaw and caused excruciating pain and slow death from hunger, due to the inability to chew. Next, a rope bit was designed to help control the horse, but it was chewed until it broke. Around this time, people had begun to extract and mold metals from the earth. The rope bit was replaced by metal and has been a curse to horses ever since, because a horse's mouth is many times more sensitive than a human's hands. Some people learned to use miniscule movements to control the reins, hence the term, "soft hands." A "hard mouth" developed if a person repeatedly pulled on the reins, which destroyed the nerves in the horse's mouth and caused the human to pull harder and more often.

"How did people learn to ride?"

"Riding horses was much more difficult than riding cattle. Sadly, men learned to ride us by breaking our spirit, if not our bones, and many died. A horse would be kept hobbled, to the point of immobility, until it was weakened. When a man mounted the hobbled horse, the horse could do nothing. Ropes would then be removed one by one. Sometimes, a horse gathered the energy to buck a person off, but most horses learned to endure the cruel treatment. Horses had certainly hoped for a more friendly relationship with humans, but would have to wait many generations before people altered their ways and worked with horses, rather than against them. Many people never learned to treat horses as conscious creatures, and to this day, continue to dominate rather than respect horses.

"Because of our strength, horses have become a symbol of power by which machines are measured and named. Your scientists say one horsepower produces more than 700 watts of energy or can move 33,000 pounds a foot per minute. In reality, every horse is different. The miniature, for example, may strain and work as hard as a huge draft and never produce one full horsepower, whereas the Clydesdale can deliver as much as 20 horsepower. People have used horses for almost every kind of work: we've skidded trees from forests to build ships that were called "wooden horses", we have built railroad tracks around the world upon which ran "iron horses." The automobile was introduced as the "horse-less carriage," and is still measured by the amount of horsepower its engine produces.

"Horses, including donkeys and mules, have packed people and their possessions thousands of miles over inhospitable terrain; we have helped humans hunt almost every kind of animal; we've pulled boats through countless canals and up many rivers; we have worked in mines and hauled out millions of tons of ore that contained gold, silver, and other precious metals. In Great Britain alone, tens of thousands of pit ponies, rarely seeing the light of day, lived and died hauling coal out of deep mines. After many premature deaths, the British Mines Act finally limited pit ponies to forty-eight hours of work per week with two weeks of annual rest. Queen Elizabeth of England stated, 'Horses should have a day off, too.' Horses loved her.

"In agriculture, especially after the invention of the padded collar, horses plowed and harvested crops that fed millions of people. We were also taught to herd domestic grazing animals. Donkeys were sometimes trained as shepherds, working on their own, to protect flocks from wolves and mountain lions. After the buffalo harvest in the American West, often just one cowboy and a few ponies—so a fresh mount was always available—herded hundreds of cattle at one time."

"What was the buffalo harvest?"

"Buffalo grazed on the North American plains for countless generations. Native Americans hunted buffalo but never threatened their existence, because the people only took what was needed and used every part of the animal. As white men pushed west across the Mississippi River, their government paid hunters to slaughter buffalo in order to clear the land for domestic cattle. Horses watched men cruelly kill tens of millions of buffalo for just their skin and tongue. The land was strewn with rotting carcasses. The stench was sickening. Buffalo were on the verge of extinction.

"Many horses also witnessed another appalling massacre—the result of another cruel invention—the barbed wire fence, which caused the mutilation and death of millions of migratory grazing animals because it hindered access to their habitats.

"As villages and towns mushroomed into cities, horses delivered building supplies, transported people, and hauled products to markets. Benjamin Franklin and his daughter Sally both loved horses. They drove from New York to Boston in a one-horse carriage to mark mileposts for the first inter-colonial highway. Four years later, a box wagon, hauled by four horses, initiated public transport between New York and Philadelphia. Nicknamed "The Flying Machine," the vehicle made the ninety-mile journey in forty-eight hours. Four- and six-team stagecoaches eventually hauled humans and their cargo across the United States.

"In 1900, London had more than four million people and four hundred thousand horses, many of whom were the first "engines" used for the city's famous double-decked busses. As the only power source for emergency vehicles, horses towed fire trucks, pulled ambulances, carried doctors to their patients, and hauled hearses.

Many cities' police forces depended on us for safety patrols and crowd control—an officer is ten times more visible on a horse than on the ground."

"Didn't the Pony Express deliver mail between Missouri and California, a distance of more than a thousand miles, in less than ten days?" I asked.

"That is true, but the first real pony express was actually organized more than two thousand years ago by the Persians," responded Bonnie.

"Genghis Khan, a leader of the Mongols, developed the largest pony express, which extended more than four thousand miles," added Lolly.

"Two thousand years ago, after the streets of Rome had been paved, mail carriers on horseback traversed the city. The cobblestones quickly wore the horses' hooves down and caused lameness, so the Romans devised hipposandals—heavy metal shoes that were tied in place with strips of leather. These became the first horseshoes," stated Sophie.

"How has the work of horses changed over the years?"

"Today, around the world, millions of horses still provide vital services for hundreds of millions of people. We till the earth for crops and transport humans and goods, as we have done for millennia. In return, our treatment varies greatly. In Vietnam, we are treated like royalty, whereas in Pakistan, we still serve as slaves.

"In some places, horses are big business. We run races, play sports, take part in shows such as rodeos and circuses, act in movies, and provide therapy and recreation for millions of people.

"The horse has been used as a logo and symbol of power to represent thousands of companies. We have had such a large impact on human society, I'll bet you can't go a full day without seeing an image of a horse on cars, clothes, television, or the movies.

"In Western medicine, tens of thousands of pregnant mares are cramped in small stalls for the collection of their urine, which is used to produce a drug for humans. Many of those mares' foals are born deformed, prematurely taken from their mothers, and the mares are impregnated again. It is a terrible job and a horrible way to live."

"How do horses benefit from domestication?"

"Some of us are fortunate enough to live with compassionate people, who provide places to bear our foals, live safely, have room to roam, and abundant fresh food and water."

"Do horses like working for humans?"

"Horses enjoy many humane jobs. Our most honorable work is using our strength to help people. We take great pleasure in working with caring people, many of whom are women."

"Who was the hardest working horse?"

"That has never concerned us. To horses, the small Shetland, some weighing less than a hundred pounds, has as much heart and works as hard as the giant Shire, who may weigh more three thousand pounds."

"Which working equine lived the longest?"

"Prudence," responded Sophie.

"Who was Prudence?"

"He was a donkey who lived sixty-three years in and around the towns of Alma and Fairplay and worked for prospectors. Settlements were built with supplies hauled by burros years before trains came to the gold mining territory of Colorado's Rocky Mountains.

"During his lifetime, Prudence, or Prunes for short, had several human companions who totally trusted him. Prunes, like other trusted donkeys, frequently went unescorted to town with a list of supplies for his human companion. The grocer would load Prunes with the goods, and he would return on his own. Rupert Sherman and Prunes were friends for more than fifty years. Mr. Sherman's final request was to be buried with his closest friend.

"The miners loved their burros and affectionately referred to them as "Rocky Mountain Canaries," for the songs they brayed. When they were too old to work, they were retired and allowed to roam free. Many women in town fed the burros. The Hand Hotel for many years made more flapjacks for burros than for people. The people of Fairplay built a monument in the center of town for Prudence, which reads:

PRUNES

A BURRO

1867 - 1930

FAIRPLAY

ALMA

ALL MINES

OF THIS

DISTRICT

"This was a dramatic contrast to the way elder horses were treated. Often we were considered a disposable commodity rather than sentient beings. When our physical usefulness waned, equines were—and still are—sold for a few dollars for slaughter to make fertilizer, glue, or food—an undignified end for loyal companions who served people their entire lives.

"Horses have accompanied people on many explorations. Without horses, Marco Polo would not have traversed the Silk Road; Lewis and Clark would have never returned from exploring the American West; and Captain Scott, who sailed to Antarctica, would never have made it to the South Pole."

"Are there places where horses are still the primary mode of transportation?"

"In many developing countries, horses are still a main mode of transport and share the road with motor vehicles. But on Mackinac Island in Lake Huron, one of the Great Lakes, the first horse-less carriage to arrive there so traumatized the working horses that local officials banned the newfangled machines. Except for emergency vehicles, Mackinac continues to solely rely on horses and bicycles.

"And there is Hydra, a small island in the Mediterranean Sea, near Athens, Greece, that goes one step further—wheeled vehicles, including bicycles, are not allowed. Water taxis are the only way to get a motorized ride around the island. Supplies brought from the mainland are transported to their final destination by horses or humans. Hydra and Mackinac have a pace of life that still resembles centuries past— the sounds of the city and crush of traffic are nonexistent—idyllic places to us."

"What has been horses' most challenging work?"

The drafts cried in unison, "WAR!"

"Can you tell me about war horses?"

"Throughout history, many brave horses have fought in man's battles. Please visit a stud stable to learn their story."

"I know of a stud farm in France. Would that be a good place to go?"

"France is the home of the courageous Marengo, Napoleon's favorite mount," mused Sophie. "Many equines there will know the stories of the horses bred for war."

"Look back at our struggle for freedom.

Trace our present day's strength to its source;

And you'll find man's pathway to glory

is strewn with the bones of a horse."

- Anonymous

WAR HORSES

The Stud Stallions; Cluny, France

The town of Cluny, located in France's Burgundy wine region, is a two hour drive west of Geneva, Switzerland. Old stone buildings line the cobblestone streets that date back to the Roman Empire. The small town has no traffic lights.

The Cluny National Stud Farm horses are stabled in four separate buildings, one of which is the second largest structure in town. It stretches the length of a football field and has ceilings more than twenty feet high.

Upon entering, I called, "Bonjour."

The closest horse whinnied a welcome. A plaque in his roomy stall indicated that his name was Ecu, an Arabian born in 1992. He was almost pure white from mane to tail. The elegant steed had a broad head, dished face, and large intelligent eyes.

I offered Ecu a carrot. He nodded toward a sign on the wall, "Ne pas nourrir les chevaux." I meekly responded that I could not read or speak French.

"It says, 'Do not feed the horses.' But it is okay. Let me try the treat."

"What about the warning?"

"I have not had carrots in a long time. You didn't put anything on them, like poison?" he asked.

"No, I would never hurt a horse."

"Good, just checking. Some crazy people harm horses for no reason. "

I gave Ecu a carrot and asked, "When was this stud stable established?"

"It dates back more than three hundred years. The emperor Napoleon needed many horses for the military and created more than thirty stud stations."

"How many stallions have reproduced here?"

"Thousands have lived here; presently there are fifty."

"What breeds are they?"

"There are several different drafts, Shires, French Trotters, Thoroughbreds, and Arabians, like myself."

"How often are you used for breeding?"

"Last year we covered more than 1,800 mares; plus there is an artificial insemination center. Veterinarians take semen from us and transport it to mares that cannot come to the stables."

"What do you mean by covered?"

"It is how horses naturally make babies. The stud mounts the mare by putting his forelegs on her back so that his erect penis can enter her vagina. After the sperm is deposited, the mare will hopefully produce a healthy baby."

"Is it the same in the wild?"

"The physical act is the same, but first, wild stallions have to court a mare to build a relationship that may last a lifetime. A female in the wild can refuse a charger if she chooses. But here, unions are prearranged."

"How do you like living here?"

"It's okay, but not great. We are treated well, but we do not get enough playtime. And unfortunately, we rarely get to meet our offspring or have romantic moments with the mares."

"Do the stallions still produce war horses?"

"Thankfully, no, though a few still partake in military ceremonies." Reading my mind, Ecu asked, "You want to know about war horses?"

"Yes, please."

Slowly shaking his head back and forth, he somberly said, "War is a very difficult subject. The history of war is long and filled with many sad stories, which need to be remembered so that future conflicts may be avoided. Tens of millions of brave horses and people have died in battle. Wars are horrific, gross, disgusting, and a disgrace to humanity."

"How did war start?"

"We really don't know, because wars began before horses became involved. War is a terrible thing—the worst invention of man. It is something horses have never really understood. No words can fully describe the brutalities. The way people slaughter each other is insane.

"Throughout history, many male animals have fought for the right to breed. We also fight over limited water or food and to protect our children or ourselves.

"But horses are dumbfounded by the wars waged by men. Almost all wars have been started and fought by males. Horses hold females in high regard. Women give life; they rarely take it."

"When were horses first used in war?"

"More than four thousand years ago, Sumerians and Assyrians used horses and cumbersome carts to haul heavily armed soldiers to battle."

"Why not use oxen?"

"An ox-drawn cart traveled only two miles per hour. Horses could haul a cart more than twice that fast. A few fresh reinforcements delivered to a strategic point, could turn the tide of a battle."

"Why did horses participate?"

"Because when we resisted, we were beaten into submission."

"Why were carts used in lieu of cavalry?"

"It was a lot safer for people to stand in a cart than to ride. Around three thousand years ago, the Hittites used lightweight spoke-wheeled chariots to great advantage. The chariot provided a platform from which archers shot arrows over their advancing army into the enemy. The use of war chariots spread across the ancient world. It was the preferred transport method used for a thousand years before horses were ridden into battle. But chariots could only be used in open, relatively flat terrain. Plus, the horses were exposed to the opposition before the men. If the horses were wounded or killed, the chariots were useless."

"Were war horses used in Asia?"

"Please ask Carlos in the next stall."

Carlos heard the query, nickered a welcome, and asked for a carrot. He was a dapple-gray Percheron, taller and broader than Ecu. His mane and tail were almond white. I gave him a treat, and he responded, "The domestic horse came to China more than five thousand years ago."

"Were chariots used in the Far East?"

"Yes, and the bit, saddle, and stirrups originated there. The largest man-made structure in history, the Great Wall of China, was built to protect people from plundering horsemen."

"Were the Chinese fond of horses?"

"Yes, Qin Shi Huang and his terra-cotta army might be the best known. The Emperor built a magnificent mausoleum for himself that contained life-sized sculptures of his personal army, which included more than seven thousand soldiers and six hundred horses. Equines are depicted more often on ancient artifacts than any other animal."

"Who were the first mounted warriors?"

"The Scythians, a nomadic people who lived the way of the horse, were the source of the Greek legend of centaurs, the half horse, half human animal. In Scythian culture, men and women were equal. Both genders were excellent riders. The legend of Amazons, women warriors who rode, stemmed from the Scythians."

"Where did they live?"

"Scythians ruled an area north of the Black Sea. On horseback, they were unmatched. They rode using a bit, but no saddle or stirrups, and were the forerunners of the Cossacks. The nomadic Scythians used equine tactics to win wars, but when they abandoned the way of the horse by creating permanent settlements, they became more vulnerable to their enemies."

"Did ancient horses admire people?"

"My buddy, Kalin, knows that answer."

Kalin was listening patiently. I offered him a carrot, which he gladly accepted. He was an Ardennais breed, a handsome, heavy draft horse with a broad, dark bay chest, black mane, and thickly feathered feet.

"Although people did not know how to properly care for us, horses liked them. Several wrote about horses, including Simon and Virgil, but our favorite was Xenophon—he really loved us," answered Kalin.

"Who was Xenophon?"

"He was from Athens and served in the army. He wrote the essay, The Art of Horsemanship, which instructed people how to compassionately care for horses. He knew that you could not properly train horses with shouts and abuse.

"Alexander the Great became Xenophon's best pupil, even though Xenophon died before Alexander was born. Alexander had access to an extensive library and learned Xenophon's text intimately. When Alexander's father, King Philip, gave Alexander the magnificent black stallion Bucephalus, the most famous friendship of ancient times between horse and human was formed."

"How did Alexander persuade Bucephalus to partake in war?"

"Alexander made the statement that many leaders use—he said he wanted to end war. Since their first major battle together resulted in no killing, the charger believed him and vowed to carry Alexander to the end of the Earth. They were together for seventeen years. Bucephalus even learned to kneel so that Alexander, in battle armor, could mount unaided. Only Alexander rode the magnificent charger, who was often injured in battle, but always protected his beloved companion. In India, after carrying Alexander to safety, Bucephalus died from wounds inflicted in battle. As Emperor, Alexander built the ancient city of Bucephala on that spot to honor his faithful friend."

"What was the next nation that relied on horses?"

"Jongleur, beside me, can tell you."

Jongleur, a solid black Ariegeois draft from the Pyrenees, happily accepted a treat. "The Romans had the next great empire that depended on equines," he answered. "First they eradicated the Italian Etruscans, a horse-loving people. The Roman Empire expanded from there, and at its height, encompassed an area where forty nations now exist."

"How important were horses for Rome?"

"The army depended heavily on the infantry, whose lifeline for reinforcements and supplies was sustained by donkeys and horses. The changeable climate sometimes rendered the dirt paths impassable for wagons. So the Romans built thousands of miles of improved stone roads to enable horses to transport goods and men in inclement conditions."

"Did the Romans have a cavalry?"

"Yes, though at first it was a minor part of their army, for when Roman horse riders arrived at a battle, they would dismount to fight. As their empire expanded, they confronted opponents who had mounted riders. So the Romans recruited cavalries from friendly or conquered tribesmen and paid mercenaries."

"Why did the Roman Empire fall?"

"One reason was that some of the emperors were deranged and neglected the State; another was their lack of equines. The enormous empire required a huge number of draft animals. Toward the end of Rome's reign, laws incorporating severe penalties were adopted to save as many horses as possible. The new laws controlled the maximum weight horses were allowed to carry or pull."

"Who had the next great equine empire?"

"Please ask Igloo," responded Jongleur.

Igloo was a Boulonnais draft horse and looked like Carlos's little brother, though he was less dappled. While enjoying his treat, he said, "After the fall of Rome, turmoil ensued for centuries. Many separate kingdoms with small cavalries were established as people migrated throughout Europe.

"Mohammed was the next leader to use horses to make a large impact on society. He unified Arabia and initiated conquests with his horsemen of Islam. The Moors' reign extended across North Africa and the Middle East and spread into Europe across the Strait of Gibraltar.

"The Franks, riding heavy war horses with stirrups imported from the Far East, defeated the Moors in France. The Arabs continued to rule in the Middle East and Africa for several hundred years."

"What was the next significant war involving horses?"

"The Battle of Hasting, between the Normans and the Saxons, was waged to determine who would rule England. The Normans had come from Scandinavia and had settled on the northwest coast of France. Led by William the Conqueror, they crossed the English Channel and invaded England with seven thousand men and almost three thousand horses.

"The larger Saxon army, led by King Harold II, lost to the Normans, because they had a cavalry, and the Saxons did not. The Norman cavalry fought using a system called the Conroy, which consisted of ten men and their horses. Fighting as a single tight-knit unit, one Conroy could usually defeat up to one hundred infantry soldiers. King Harold II was killed during the fighting, and William the Conqueror became the next King of England. Mounted feudal knights on large, heavy horses became the most feared and successful warriors."

"Why did war horses need to be bigger?"

"The great war horses of Europe had to be larger and sturdier, because a feudal knight's armor, combined with a horse's armor, weighed almost 300 pounds. A heavily armored soldier could not lift himself onto a horse without help.

"During the Crusades, knights from France and Germany rode war horses over a thousand miles to rout the Islamic horsemen and claim the Holy Land in the Middle East. Some of the horses' front hooves were shod with protruding, stud-like nails to trample the enemy. Sadly, horses inadvertently became killing weapons."

"Were there any other great dynasties that depended on equines?"

"Ask Lupin, behind you," answered Igloo.

Lupin gratefully accepted his carrot. He was quite tall, but slender; his shiny coat was coal black. He stated, "Temujin, or Genghis Khan, united the separate tribes of Mongolian horsemen. With a relatively small army, they created the largest land empire on Earth. It stretched almost six thousand miles from the Pacific Ocean to the Black Sea.

"The Khan's army had four times as many horses as men, which ensured that the cavalry always had fresh mounts when they rode into battle. Plus, they employed tactics with the horse, such as the feigned withdrawal the Scythians devised.

"The Mongolians used bits, saddles, and stirrups, could ride for days, and only dismounted to change horses. In an emergency, soldiers would pierce a horse's neck vein, to drink blood for nourishment, while remaining in the saddle. The Khan and his soldiers were fierce, brutal, and unmatched in combat. But the enormous empire did not last long, because being nomadic, the Mongolians seldom left occupying forces behind. When their leader died, it was customary to return home to bury the ruler. Forty of the best stallions and mares from Genghis' personal pure white herd of ten thousand were killed and interred with the great Khan."

"Were there other cavalries in the Orient?"

"The Samurai of Japan were extraordinary warriors. They could slice a man and a horse in two with one pass of the sword. A Japanese proverb claims that a Samurai's child awakens to the sound of the bridle. Before people from the West appeared, horses were sacred, only ridden by royalty or Samurai, and never used to draw carts or wagons."

"In one of Shakespeare's plays, someone said, 'A horse! A horse! My kingdom for a horse!' Did someone actually speak those words?" I asked.

"King Richard III made that call for help after being thrown from his horse while fighting for the crown of England. He was England's last king to die in battle. This war was also the end of heavy armor and the larger war horse, because the Chinese had invented gunpowder and created crude guns and cannons. As those weapons became more reliable, armor and the heavy horse became obsolete."

"Did horses affect the outcome of other wars?"

"Please ask Flambeau," answered Lupin.

Flambeau lightly pawed the ground, politely asking for a treat. He was a beautiful black Percheron weighing over a ton. He thanked me for the carrot and answered, "Around five hundred years ago, Europeans were producing sailing ships large enough to navigate oceans. Christopher Columbus crossed the Atlantic in search of a shorter trade route to the Far East. Landing on a Caribbean island off the coast of the Americas, he discovered the New World. On a later trip, Columbus brought thirty-four horses.

"The equines were happy to be returning to the land of their origin. They looked forward to seeing their brethren after thousands of years of separation. But crossing the Atlantic was an arduous journey. The horses were bound and severely restricted—more than half perished. Part of the ocean was named the "horse latitudes," because so many horses' bodies were tossed overboard and floated in the sea. After we arrived, to our great dismay, we discovered that our indigenous relatives had either perished or emigrated long ago.

"Then Cortes, a Spaniard, with less than fifty men and sixteen horses, challenged the Aztec Empire of more than a million people. Cortes and his fearful men rode their horses down the beach while firing their guns. The Aztecs had never encountered horses or guns. Some even thought the invaders were gods. Cortes' soldiers credited their great victory to the horses.

"When Cortes rode into the Aztec capital city, he declared it the most beautiful place he had ever seen. Less than ten years later, the conquered Aztec Empire lay in ruins.

"A few years later, the Spaniard, Francisco Pizarro, landed in Peru. With one hundred infantry and sixty cavalry, he faced the Incas, the largest empire in the New

World. The small Spanish force confronted eighty thousand Incan warriors. Pizarro tricked the Incan leaders into gathering for peace talks, and then slaughtered them without losing a single one of his own soldiers.

"The Europeans unwittingly unleashed an even more terrible scourge—disease. War and ensuing sieges in Europe led to livestock and people living in close proximity, which created a breeding ground for deadly viruses. Millions of people in Europe perished due to plagues, but the people who survived developed resistance. When the New World's native peoples were exposed to those germs, they were defenseless; unfortunately nearly nineteen of the twenty million indigenous inhabitants died.

"Some lucky horses escaped and flourished, because they had no natural predators. They spread across the Americas. Some horses lived with indigenous Indians, whom the horses dearly loved, because they were treated with respect, like brothers and sisters. Horses dwelt in harmony with the Indians for many generations, renewing their hope for better days."

"What happened to the horses in Europe?"

"European cavalry horses were bred to be quick and maneuverable, while the large draft horses hauled ammunition, cannons, and supplies. No one took better advantage of this than Napoleon Bonaparte, the Emperor of France.

"Napoleon had more than a thousand horses in his personal herd. His favorite was a white Arab named Marengo. The diminutive emperor liked smaller horses because they made him look bigger. Nearly twenty horses were shot out from under Napoleon during battle. Marengo received five bullet wounds during fights, but eventually outlived his master."

"What happened to Napoleon?"

"The Emperor fought across Europe all the way to Moscow. The Russians abandoned the city and disappeared into the vast grasslands to avoid the enemy. During his return to France, Napoleon lost tens of thousands of men and horses from the bitter cold winter. He was ultimately defeated at the Battle of Waterloo. That was a terrible day—fifty thousand men and twenty thousand horses died."

"Was that the end of mounted warfare?"

"Regrettably, no. I will let Gouverneur continue the story."

I turned toward Gouverneur and had to look up to make eye contact. He was a gray Percheron and the tallest horse in the stable. His gentle demeanor was evident as he bowed his head for me to massage his poll. I gave Gouverneur a carrot that he nibbled slowly, then said, "In America's Civil War, more than one and a half million equines lost their lives. Horses, donkeys, and mules carried cavalry, urgent dispatches, mail, and the news. They hauled artillery, guns, and munitions to the battlefields and carted away the injured. Plus they pulled countless miles of wagon trains filled with supplies."

"How were the horses treated?"

"The generals who recognized our value treated us the best. A person's status is elevated more than just physically when seated upon a horse. Anyone standing on the ground has to look up to a rider, who assumes a commanding and regal presence.

"Robert E. Lee's favorite horse, Traveller, was almost as well known to Confederate soldiers as their commanding general. Ulysses S. Grant, the military commander of the Union Army, who was later elected President of the United States, knew the worth of horses. Once, before a major battle, he observed an attendant abusing a horse. He had the soldier tied to a tree for six hours as punishment for animal cruelty.

"After the war ended, the U.S. Army was organized to fight Indians and to clear western lands for white settlers. This upset the horses, who were proud to be the Indians' companions, because the indigenous people lived in harmony with the Earth and always treated horses with respect. Such a relationship was what horses had envisioned when partnering with people. Many Indian cultures were brutally and senselessly eradicated by the overwhelming numbers of white soldiers. The remaining Indians were relegated to reservations and prohibited from possessing horses."

"Did horses participate in war during the twentieth century?"

"Horses carried on bravely through many wars, including the Boer, the Spanish-American, and World Wars I and II. Sadly, millions of horses and people died in those wars."

"Who was the bravest horse?"

Snorting filled the air. Gouveneur's voice rose above the din, "We don't distinguish one from another regarding bravery. Any horse that has gone to war is a brave horse, and any horse that comes home is a hero and deserves a life of leisure. But there is a story that demonstrates the extent to which an equine will go for humans. I relate it in the hope that more men will respect equines for their intelligence and compassion and treat us accordingly.

"Abdul was a donkey, Egyptian by birth. He was a small, hardworking equine who was called into service by the Australians during World War I. Abdul hauled water to the front for the fighting soldiers, then carried the wounded to the rear in a seemingly, never ending circle.

"During one vicious battle at Gallipoli, Turkey, Abdul's human partner was killed. To the amazement of the men, Abdul carried on with his tasks, unescorted, for long hours after the sun had set. The brave, little donkey inspired the soldiers to persevere even at death's doorstep."

I slowly shook my head in grief.

"Do you have any other questions?"

"Who was the most famous war horse?"

Gouveneur said to ask Ecu.

I had unwittingly circled the stable and was again standing beside the handsome Arabian. I gave him another carrot. He was happy that everyone was able to share the treats. He spoke musingly, "Perhaps the most famous war horse was not even real, but nevertheless, determined the outcome of a ten-year war in one day.

"The war was fought more than three thousand years ago. After ten years, both sides had lost many men, and no end was in sight. Leaders from the army that lay siege withdrew in their ships. They left behind a symbol to their gods—a giant effigy of a horse.

"When the sun rose the next day, the people inside the fortress thought that the enemy had finally given up and retreated. They claimed the magnificent work of art as their own and brought it within the protected walls of the city. That night, they held a huge celebration. In the early morning hours, the men returned from their feigned withdrawal. Soldiers, hidden inside the huge horse, descended from its belly and opened the city's gates. The invaders poured in, killed most of the people, and destroyed the city of Troy.

"The huge wooden horse came to be known as the Trojan Horse. It is the most famous war horse and has become a symbol of trickery and deceit."

"Why is it that you all know so much about war?"

"The horses here have lots of free time to review our history."

"Then any one of you could have told me the story of war horses?"

Snorts and whinnies of laughter filled the air. "Don't feel bad. We just led you in a circle to ensure that everyone got a carrot."

I laughed aloud and asked, "Do horses still fight in wars?"

"Unfortunately, yes, and with your new technologies, war is more dangerous than ever. This is another reason why we want to empower women. Women leaders would be much less apt to go to war than men, which would make our world a safer place for everyone, horses included. With more women leaders, we would have extra time for our favorite form of play."

"What is that?"

"Racing! We love to run!" Several horses neighed in agreement.

"Well, who was the fastest horse?"

"You need to meet Jigor's cousin, Legend. He is a Thoroughbred who lives at Stall Richardson in Frankfurt, Germany, not far from here."

I circled the stable once more to dispense the remaining carrots and thanked my new friends before heading to Germany.

"Horse sense is the thing a horse has which keeps it from betting on people."

- W. C. FIELDS

RACE HORSES

Legend; Frankfurt, Germany

The drive to Frankfurt passed quickly, as I recalled the time I watched Secretariat thunder down the home stretch at Belmont racetrack. With an incredible thirty length lead, the steed seemed to be running a separate race. In 1978, Secretariat won the Triple Crown —horse racing's greatest prize.

The trolley to the Rehn Bahn racetrack meandered through the old city and crossed the Rhine River. Structures standing side by side, built hundreds of years apart, reflected constantly changing architectural styles.

Making my way around the racing oval to Stall Richardson, I passed an abandoned starting gate, its paint peeling away. Next to it stood a rusted wheelbarrow overflowing with old twisted horseshoes. A golf course in the infield seemed absurd—a wildly struck ball could cause serious injury to horse or rider.

The stable was bustling with activity. A girl, with brushes in hand, asked me to wait in the jockeys' lounge, since Mr. Richardson was very protective of the horses.

The lounge was a converted horse stall. Lockers were crammed around a table, and a bulletin board was filled with notes about the horses and upcoming races. I laid out sweets for the staff while waiting to visit Legend.

When Mr. Richardson entered, he introduced himself as Dave. He inquired about the cakes and thanked me. Surmising the bag of carrots was for the horses, he requested that I give them out after training.

I asked Dave about Legend. He smiled and said, "I really like that horse. He seems to be everyone's favorite. All the training jockeys want to ride him. Legend's owners have six horses here, but he is their favorite, too. Legend's only problem is that he has not won a race. Please, try not to mention that."

Dave said that Legend's training jockey today would be Nicola. He pointed toward his stall and noted that Legend liked to be stroked, like a cat. Dave then excused himself to prepare the horses for their training session.

The stalls were spacious. A small sign on each door listed the horse's name, year of birth, lineage, and owner. Legend was born in 1999; Monsun, his sire, and Lorchen, his mother. Legend was gazing out his window at the track when I introduced myself. He turned and welcomed me with a nicker. He was magnificent and muscular, with a beautiful chestnut coat, a white star on his handsome face, and a lovely black forelock. He stood tall and proud—every bit the epitome of a legend. He approached and sniffed my hand. After a few moments, I lightly rubbed his nose, and we exchanged telepathic greetings. He nuzzled my ear then tickled my neck. I laughed aloud.

I related greetings from the chargers at Cluny. Surprised, Legend asked, "How is my cousin, Jigor?"

"He is happy and very healthy," I replied and asked, "How do you like staying at Stall Richardson and racing at Renn Bahn?"

"Any Thoroughbred would like Stall Richardson. We are treated very well. It is the best stable at the track. The only problem is there is no place to run free. When

I gallop around unencumbered, my stride is longer, and I run faster. The only time I run here is when somebody is on my back. There used to be paddocks in the middle of the track where we could socialize, run around unimpeded, and play. But now, a golf course is there. Dave is aware of the problem, but I think opportunities to run free would help me win."

"How do you like your owners?" I asked, avoiding any reference to his race record.

"They are very nice people, doing everything they can, even skipping vacations to save money for my care. When I am not in training, I visit their farm. They have large paddocks where I can play and run all day with other horses. I love their open pastures and hope to retire there."

"Do you like Mr. Richardson?"

"Dave is the best man I have ever met. He treats horses like they were his children, and he is very patient. Patience is the key to success with horses. Dave was an outstanding professional jockey."

"Here in Frankfurt?"

"Dave grew up and rode in England before coming to Germany. His first time out here he won the German Derby—the biggest horse race in the country. Dave won the Derby twice more, as well as hundreds of other races. Once, when Be My Wish was seriously injured, he stayed up all night nursing the horse. Several people, including a veterinarian, wanted to put her down. Thanks to Dave, she fully recovered."

"Do you like horse racing?"

"Human-horse racing is all right, and I like my companions. Plus, the people here treat horses with respect. I just wish I could win a race." Legend sadly dipped his head, scraped the ground with a hoof, and continued, "One time I led most of the way but finished second. That was my best result. Maybe in a shorter race, I could win. It's hard to live up to my name."

"Are horses very competitive?"

Legend perked up and responded, "We love to run! Sometimes we even race the wind. Galloping with total abandon is exhilarating.

"In the wild, families and bachelor bands exercise to enhance everyone's strength, because bands can only run together as fast as the slowest member. The fastest horses usually live the longest. In nature, we race to survive. Here, the majority of Thoroughbreds would prefer not to win human-horse races, because winning brings more responsibilities, bigger races, and more weight to carry."

"Have any horses in this stable won a race?"

"Dave's horses have a great race record."

Just then, a horse and a groom walked by. The mare was as tall as Legend but slightly darker. She whinnied enthusiastically at us.

"That's Royal Samantha; she won her last race," Legend stated proudly.

I congratulated Royal Samantha, then asked Legend about his training regimen.

"First, I am groomed. Do you know who my training jockey is today?"

"Dave mentioned Nicola."

"Great, I love Nicola. I like having a female training partner. It is rare to have women in horse racing, but Dave is very perceptive and sees that the horses respond well to care from females."

"Have you ever raced with a woman jockey?"

"No, unfortunately."

"Why?"

"At first, organized human-horse racing was one method used by men to keep women down. For many years, men used the excuse of personal safety to exclude women from racing. In truth, a woman on a horse becomes an equal to any man in the saddle, and superior to a man on the ground. Not letting women compete was one way to keep them subservient."

"What happens next in your training day?"

"Nicola checks my body to make sure I am healthy. While brushing me, she inspects my skin, ensures that my legs are warm, and examines my hooves. After tacking me up, Nicola will mount, and we go see Dave. We circle him, as he closely inspects each of us. Sometimes, he asks questions and gives special instructions to a jockey. Then we head out for training.

"Dave watches us closely with binoculars from the grandstand. The first time around the track, we are warmed up at a trotting pace. On the second lap, we run up to ninety percent of full speed. The third time, we slow to cool down. Five or six times a week, we gallop very hard for a minute or two."

"How long is the track?"

"It's one mile around."

Legend continued, "Then I return to my stall where my jockey removes the tack. I am brushed down and taken to an automatic walker. I walk at a comfortable pace, until Dave determines that I am properly cooled. Then, I am thoroughly soaped, washed, and dried. I walk around Dave again as he inspects me. Once back in my room, I am groomed, given food, and allowed to drink.

"Dave tries to recognize every nuance of a horse's condition. If he sees the slightest moisture in a horse's nostril, he changes the feed slightly and provides vitamins. He will also schedule a checkup with the veterinarian."

"How often are you raced?"

"About once every three weeks. Most horses at other stables are run more frequently, but Dave is very cautious. He knows racing, especially on long courses, can be very hard on horses."

When Nicola entered Legend's stall, he nickered loudly to express his joy. She gave him a huge hug and brushed him down. Legend loved Nicola's attention. He attempted to return the favor by gently grooming her back with his teeth. She laughed at his playfulness.

Following Legend and Nicola through the stable, I scanned the horses' name plates and greeted them as we passed. They included: Touchdown, Victory's Pleasure, Right Now, Tiger Valley, Kaisertraum, Stanhope, Sign of Nike (he had a swoosh on his forehead like Nike's logo), Spatzolita, and Angelero. They all looked like world-class athletes.

Outside, I asked Nicola, "How long have you been riding?"

With a beaming smile, she said, "I started riding when I was six and feel very lucky to be a training jockey for Mr. Richardson. I get paid modestly and have to work another full-time job to pay my living expenses. To work here requires that I am up very early, but I would not miss this experience for the world. I love horses and the feel of their power while racing around the track."

Nicola asked for a leg up. I intertwined my fingers as a platform for Nicola's shin and lifted her as she swung her right leg over Legend, gently settling into the saddle. They joined five other horses and circled around Dave, before getting the nod to head for the track.

Dave invited me to accompany him to the grandstand to watch the horses run. The view encompassed the track, the golf course, and the city's skyline. The horses trotted in single file at an easy pace. Dave studied each horse carefully. By the second lap, the horses were running hard. Dave was now in the horses' world, intently watching the Thoroughbreds' beautiful, galloping strides. Their speed seemed effortless. Hooves pounded the track as clods of turf flew through the air. The jockeys rocked in synchronicity with their horses. Even the golfers paused to admire them flying by. While studying the horses, Dave said, "If a horse is enjoying the training, his ears are up and moving about. If they are laid flat back, he is unhappy."

"Why would a horse not enjoy training?"

"Horses are individuals, and Thoroughbreds are a delicate breed. Training for horse racing can be arduous. More than ninety percent of a horse's behavior and performance problems have to do with pain. A good trainer needs to know each horse's tendencies to keep them all as healthy as possible." The horses were trotting again, and Dave keenly watched them cool down. We then returned to the stables to greet the horses and jockeys.

Back at his stall, I asked Legend, "How did you like training today?"

"There has been no rain for weeks so the track is too dry, which makes the turf soft and hard to run on. Plus, people mix sand with the earth, which creates dust that makes it difficult to breathe. But I'd rather run on turf than dirt any day. It is easier on my legs when galloping hard." Legend then took a long drink from his automatically-filled water bowl.

A groom brought Legend's dinner. While he feasted heartily, I retrieved the carrots from the lounge and passed them out to the Thoroughbreds. Dave said that he had several appointments that afternoon, but that I could stay with the horses. Legend was pleasantly surprised with the treats. When he finished, I asked, "When did horse racing begin?"

Whinnying, snorting, and even a bray that could have come from a burro filled the air, as the horses laughed at my question. Legend answered, "Horses have run races for millions of years. Long ago, Dawn persuaded equines to switch, from remaining camouflaged in the dense forests to outrunning predators on the open prairie, for survival. Running races became our favorite form of play. In the wild, racing is the training for our continued existence. Living in close proximity to predators, a horse that cannot gallop fast will not live long. I love a quick head to head sprint across an open pasture."

"How far can wild horses run?"

"Most all-out races are dashes of usually less than a quarter mile, because we are practicing to outrun predators. At a slower pace, wild horses can run for hours and cover up to forty miles in a day."

"When did people start racing horses?"

"Human-horse racing began soon after people started riding horses. People have been racing with horses ever since. For five thousand years, the fastest mode of travel for a person was on the back of a horse. We are the only animals, besides people, to compete in the Olympics."

"When did horses first compete in the Games?"

"Almost three thousand years ago, horses pulled chariots in the Greek games. A hundred years later, riding events were added."

"What type of racing do equines like least?"

"The steeplechase," answered Legend. "Only a small number of horses enjoy leaping; we only jump to please people or to escape a predator. If we were given the choice of running around or leaping over obstacles in our path, we would skirt them; jumping is a last resort."

"Why do you jump for people?"

"Because of the unwritten rule—You take care of me and I take care of you. Horses jump in return for food, water, and kind companionship. Horses love to build relationships that lead to lasting friendships."

"Please tell me more about the steeplechase."

"Steeplechase racecourses are tough; several miles long, with many obstacles for a horse to leap. All human-horse racing is hazardous, but the steeplechase frequently subjects horses to grave risk. Taking off and landing puts extraordinary pressure on our legs. An injury sustained in a race may mean the end of life for an unlucky horse. Human-horse racing can be dangerous for jockeys too; both horses and riders have died while racing.

"The premier horse racing event in England is the grueling Grand National, a steeplechase run annually at the Aintree track. In one race, thirty-six horses started; three were killed, and only six managed to finish. At another Grand National, twenty-eight horses balked or fell at a single fence."

"What are the barriers made of, and how high are they?"

"Fences vary; some are post and rail, others earthen banks, or rows of hedges. They are from two to six feet high. The takeoff and landing areas may vary, which increases each jump's difficulty significantly. A few of the hurdles are combined with water hazards. Equines have a small blind spot in front of the nose that makes it tough to gauge a jump."

"When was the first steeplechase?"

"The first was in Ireland almost three hundred years ago. It was run between two churches with high steeples, which were prominent landmarks."

"Who was the greatest steeplechase racer?"

"Lottery," replied Touchdown, from an adjoining stall. "He was a Grand National champion, a tall horse that could trot faster than most horses could gallop. He won so many races, that for several years, open races were advertised as, 'Open to all horses except Lottery.'

"He was one horse that really loved to leap and liked to show off. If given the opportunity, he would effortlessly jump his owner's lunch table and leave everything untouched."

"What about Red Rum?" snorted Stanhope. "He was the only three-time winner of the English Grand National. After he passed away, Red Rum was laid to rest at the track's finish line." Several of the horses whinnied their respect.

"Which was the greatest steeplechase race?"

"It was run in France by Mandarin, and jockey, Fred Winter. At the fourth fence, Mandarin's rubber bit broke, leaving Fred powerless. All he could do was hang on. Mandarin successfully negotiated the twenty-six remaining jumps, then bolted to the lead to win in a desperate finish."

"Do people still race chariots?"

"Chariots and wagons pulled by teams of horses are still raced in many places. But, for a single horse, pacing or trotting while towing a feather-light sulky is more popular now."

"What's the difference between pacing and trotting?"

"Both are two-beat gaits. In pacing, both legs on the same side of the body move together. A pacer is nicknamed a "side-wheeler." Trotting is accomplished by moving the front and the opposite rear leg in unison."

"Which is harder for a horse?"

"Pacing has to be taught, but once it is mastered, it is easier to run with speed. Trotting comes naturally to horses; it is a common stride we use in the wild. But trotting at top speed can be extremely difficult. A horse that breaks its gait, even for a single step, has to drop to the rear of the pack or is disqualified from the race."

"Do horses run both gaits?"

"A horse is trained to race only one."

"Who was the best pacer?"

"It was Dan Patch," whinnied Indian Point. "The Patch never lost a race. The pacer and his kind, caring companion, Mr. Savage, formed a lifelong relationship. Dan Patch was recognized across America, because he traveled in a private boxcar and stopped to put on shows. Many children wished for a Dan Patch hobbyhorse as a birthday gift. In one race, more than one hundred thousand people gathered to watch him run. Years later, when his owner was in the hospital for minor surgery, he was told of The Patch's passing. His dedicated owner died the following day."

"Which is faster, pacing or trotting?"

"Pacing is slightly faster than trotting. But trotting has a larger following."

"Then who was the greatest trotter?"

"The champion, Greyhound," answered Stanhope. "He was nicknamed The Grey Ghost. He established racing records that held for more than thirty years. He was the king of trotters."

"Well then, Rosalind was the queen." Royal Samantha retorted. "Rosalind lived at the same time and had almost as many victories. They were well matched and once set a world record running together. They were the royalty of the trotting world."

"Which type of human-horse race is your favorite?"

"The Pack Burro Triple Crown," answered Touchdown. "It is comprised of three, long distance races in Buena Vista, Fairplay, and Leadville, Colorado. The courses are nearly twenty miles long and are run through the mountains."

"Why is it your favorite?"

"Because people have to run beside the burros; no riding is allowed. A person is tethered to his equine partner, who carries a pick, shovel, gold pan, and water. People get to experience what running is like for the racehorse."

"Which form of horse racing is the most popular today?"

"Human-horse racing is big business—millions of people bet billions of dollars on the thousands of races held each year. Today, Thoroughbred racing is the most popular. There are Thoroughbred races in more than a hundred countries. Thoroughbreds are also the most expensive racehorses to buy, because they run for the richest prizes, worth millions of dollars," stated Legend.

"Why are Thoroughbreds so prized?"

"The breed, Thoroughbred, only applies to horses eligible for *The Thoroughbred Stud Book*, which requires that a horse's ancestry includes one of three sires: Byerly Turk, Darley Arabian, or Godolphin Barb."

"They were the first Thoroughbreds?"

"The foundation horses, Arabian stallions bred to British and European mares, produced larger and stronger horses that could carry weight at good speed over a long distance."

"How is *The Thoroughbred Stud Book* used?"

"It traces a horse's lineage and guides people to breed the best with the best. It also helps buyers gauge how much to spend on a potential winner. Many factors are involved in producing a winning steed; ancestry is one. Most great horses are born, not made. Many impressive racers never became champions, due to unsympathetic trainers and a lack of attention to the horses' care."

"Which Thoroughbred had the best support group?"

"There are many caring individuals in the horse racing world. One of the best entourages was Seabiscuit's. "The Biscuit" was an over-raced three-year-old, when he was sold to the Howards. Seabiscuit was contemptuous of racing, since he had already run a career's worth.

"The Howards did everything they could for Seabiscuit and gave his trainer, Tom Smith, free rein. Tom provided Seabiscuit with several animal friends in order to help the horse rebuild his trust in people: a sweet little mare, Pumpkin; a dog, Pocatell; and a spider monkey, JoJo. The wall between Seabiscuit's stall and Pumpkin's was removed, so that the gang could share a large space and sleep together.

"Mr. Smith exercised great patience in working with Seabiscuit. So did the jockey, Red Pollard. Seabiscuit responded to their loving care by winning races in record time. He ignited the horse racing world. While Mr. Howard was negotiating a race between the undefeated Triple Crown winner, War Admiral, and Seabiscuit, Pollard was seriously injured. Though Red could not ride the Biscuit in the famous match race, he made sure that the substitute jockey understood every nuance about the horse.

"With millions of people listening on the radio, Seabiscuit won the dramatic race in front of a huge crowd on War Admiral's home track. Then, during the world's richest horse race, the Santa Anita Handicap, Seabiscuit was injured. Many veterinarians thought that he would never race again. His loving team gave the steed all the time he needed to heal. Seabiscuit, with Red aboard, returned to racing and won the Handicap. If more men treated their horses with the same love and respect as Seabiscuit's team, horse racing results would surely improve."

"What is the most important quality for a trainer?"

"Patience is the key to successful horse training. Most Thoroughbreds are started too young. Many owners demand quick results and do unscrupulous things to make a horse go faster or slower."

"Why make a horse go slower?"

"So the horse loses. In the early days of organized horse racing, most races were head to head, or match, races. Sometimes, the night before a race, a man would stealthily sneak into an opponent's stable and take the horse out for a long, hard ride. The next day, the weary horse would lose the race. Men have done many other disgusting tricks to make us run faster or slower. Sea Cottage was shot in the rump so he couldn't run—but he was a horse with great heart and won the race anyway. In another instance, an attendant was paid to make his horse lose. He ground ping pong balls into a fine powder and forced the horse to inhale it. The dust made it very difficult for the horse to breathe and caused him to lose the race.

"Too much racing is another way to ruin great horses. Miss Cheyenne was forced to run sixteen races in twenty-one days. There are just too many sad stories to tell."

"What have people done to make equines run faster?"

"There are many speed substances that make us run harder. Once, while a trainer was feeding his horse a few "speedy" sugar cubes, the track's chief steward confronted him. The trainer tried to show that the sugar was harmless—he consumed a cube and gave one to the race judge. The trainer's final instruction to the jockey was, 'Let the horse run, and if you hear anyone coming up from behind you, do not look back, as it will be either the judge or me.' " Several horses whinnied in derisive laughter.

"Sometimes, jockeys were also guilty of cheating. Before cameras and patrol judges were used, some jockeys would do almost anything to win. They would yank an opposing horse's tail or pull its tack to slow a horse. Some jockeys actually exchanged punches during races. Today, Thoroughbreds are tested for drugs, so it is harder to dope a horse, but cheating still occurs. Some horses have even been kidnapped. Shergar, winner of the English Derby, was stolen from his stable. A ten million dollar ransom was demanded for his safe return. Before the owners could make a deal, the kidnappers killed the famous horse."

"Which was the greatest horse race?"

"Before the invention of the photo finish, the Gravesend Racetrack, in New York, employed racing judges to determine the winners. There was a race between Bing Aman and Marr Jordan, two evenly matched horses, who highly admired one another. They dashed around the track, switching the lead, but crossed the finish line tied. The race was re-run. Amazingly, it was another dead heat. The third running was also ruled a draw. The fourth time they passed under the finish line, the fatigued horses again appeared tied, but the judges awarded the win, by a nose, to Bing Aman. The crowd protested so riotously that the track was destroyed."

"Who was the fastest of all racehorses?"

"Who do you think?"

"Secretariat," I blurted out.

Several snorts filled the air. "Secretariat was a great horse. He won sixteen out of twenty-one races. Secretariat and Phar Lap, two of the best ever Thoroughbreds, had enlarged hearts—almost twice their normal size."

"Who was Phar Lap?"

"He was Australia's greatest racehorse. Phar Lap, which means lightning in the Thai language, was born in New Zealand. He was brought to Australia and formed a very close relationship with an attendant, Tommy Woodcock. Phar Lap was trained very hard, and when the groom protested, he was fired. Phar Lap refused to eat until Tommy was rehired. The groom loved Phar Lap so much that he used his own body as a shield when gunmen tried to assassinate the horse.

"It took a while for Phar Lap to understand the human-horse racing game. After losing his first four starts, he won thirty-seven of forty-seven races, including the Melbourne Cup, Australia's most prestigious horse race. Phar Lap once won fourteen races in a row, including four in eight days. After he was shipped to America, Phar Lap won again, but died mysteriously a few days later when he was just six years old."

"How did he die?"

"We do not know; it might have been infected feed or something sinister."

"Was there ever an undefeated Thoroughbred?"

"Eclipse, a great, great-grandson of Darley Arabian, never lost a race. He was so fast that jockeys never had to spur or whip him to encourage him. He was foaled during a total eclipse of the sun and was famous in England. Eighty percent of modern Thoroughbreds have Eclipse in their pedigree."

"Was Eclipse the fastest horse?"

"No, some quarter horses have sprinted faster—up to fifty-five miles per hour. But all of us can gallop faster when not carrying a person. The fastest horse was never ridden, though many men tried to capture him. He roamed through Europe and Asia thousands of years ago. The charger was snow-white and so fast that when galloping, his streaming mane looked like wings, so he appeared to be flying. No one beat him in a race. No one was even close. You call him Pegasus."

"Pegasus was real?"

"Horses never lie," Legend stated simply.

"If you could be another type of horse, what would you be?"

"I would be a Lipizzaner stallion at the Spanish Riding School. They are the world's finest performance horses. They are superbly cared for and are not pressured by competition. The Lipizzaners get to run around, race, and play together in huge rolling pastures. They are able, and encouraged, to form intimate relationships with kind people. Their main home is in Vienna."

"Why is it called the Spanish Riding School if it is located in Austria?"

"You need to ask the Lipizzaners," sighed Legend wistfully.

"I believe there is some kind of sixth sense

between human and animal."

- GARY STEVENS

PERFORMANCE HORSES

Europa; Vienna, Austria

Driving southeast from Frankfurt, along the Danube River, I passed through a pristine valley with thick forests blanketing the foothills. Suny's story, about ancient herds of wild horses following the river, came to mind. At the German-Austrian border, the Danube flowed east, the road turned south, and the famous Austrian Alps pierced the horizon.

My hotel was located in Vienna's Altstadt, or Old City. The friendly staff encouraged me to explore the city on foot. They directed me to the Imperial Palace, where the Spanische Reitschule, or Spanish Riding School, was located. I ambled along slowly to admire the diverse, intricately detailed architecture of this culturally rich city—home of Mozart, Beethoven, Brahms, Hayden, Schubert, and Strauss.

The Imperial Palace was huge. It took twenty minutes just to find the equestrian entrance, which was located in a courtyard graced by an imposing statue of an emperor astride a charger. The woman in the administration office was sympathetic to my mission and the horses' cause but said that public performances to see the Lipizzaners were sold out three months in advance.

She sensed my disappointment, asked me to wait, and made a call. After a few minutes of conversing, she asked me to return to the office at eight the next morning. I nodded enthusiastically, gave her a business card, and thanked her profusely. She said that Johann Riegler, Chief Trainer of the Spanish Riding School, would meet me.

The next morning, I met a gentleman sporting a two-cornered, gold-braided hat with the broad side facing forward; a double-breasted brown waistcoat with two rows of gold buttons and long tails; white buckskin trousers; and knee-high, black leather boots. After a firm handshake, he said, "I am Johann Riegler; please call me Hans. You are writing a book for horses?"

"Yes, sir."

"Good. I want to introduce you to Europa, who is like my brother. We talk all the time. In the greatest equestrian arena in the world, we will show you the harmony that exists between two true companions," he stated proudly.

Hans led me to the Royal Box. Situated on the ground, it felt as though I could reach out and touch the horses. It was filled with plush, deep purple velvet chairs. Before sitting, I asked, "May I give Europa a few carrots?"

"I'm sorry, but the steeds' diets are closely monitored. No one from the outside may feed the stallions." Then he whispered, "Give me a couple, and I will give them to Europa. I will tell him they are from you."

Except for the sandy floor, the hippodrome was like a grand ballroom. Enormous chandeliers illuminated the fifty-foot high, white, wooden-walled hall. Columns and intricately carved archways supported the ceiling. The cavernous hall was empty except for a portrait of Emperor Karl VI astride a steed. The Emperor had had the magnificent riding arena constructed in 1735. I absorbed the history, and settled deeper into the plush grandeur of the Royal Box.

Suddenly, symphonic music filled the air. Hans entered astride Europa, a beautiful Lipizzaner stallion with a strong arched neck, small ears, and expressive dark eyes. His body was white; his powerful legs dappled gray. They paused to salute the Emperor's image before beginning the practice performance.

For the next hour, the pair performed numerous maneuvers including spectacular leaps. Two moved as one; Europa and Hans seemed suspended in air at times. Hans remained perfectly balanced on Europa without the aid of stirrups. The elegant, graceful stallion waltzed to a Mozart minuet, then displayed a smooth trot with high leg action while moving forward at a walking pace. The evident harmony between horse and human created an amazing display. At the end, I gave them a spontaneous standing ovation.

After the performance, Hans escorted me to the immaculate stables. Spacious stalls divided by waist-high walls allowed the stallions to see one another. Attendants and riders busily prepared the horses for a public practice. Hans introduced me to Europa, then left to arrange the morning training session. Cordial Europa promptly thanked me for the carrots.

I asked, "How do you like being a performing Lipizzaner?"

"I am retired from public performances. What you saw was pure pleasure."

"It was beautiful! How old are you?"

"Twenty-two."

"You look great."

Europa raised his head high, struck a statuesque pose, and responded, "Thank you. Hans and the grooms take great care of me."

"How long did you do public performances?"

"For ten years."

"What do you do now?"

"I am a schooling stallion—I teach the young riders."

"You are their teacher?"

"Yes, some horses here serve as instructors. A four-legged teacher is sometimes more important than the two-legged ones. Every schooling stallion here has deposited students onto the soft sand," Europa nickered.

"How do you give lessons?"

"A balanced rider feels sensations that cannot be described by a human instructor. The proper seat has to be experienced to be understood. Every horse and rider pairing is unique. A balanced pair has freedom of movement that can be exhilarating. I have taught many young riders a proper seat."

"Was Mr. Riegler always your trainer?"

"I have worked with others, but not in a long time. Hans is like a brother."

"What happens when you stop teaching?"

"Hans promised he would always care for me. My father, Europa Sr., also one of Hans' pupils, performed for the public then spent the last years of his life at Hans' home."

"Where did you grow up?"

"On the Lipizzaner Piper, the official stud stables for the Spanish Riding School, in the country one hundred miles away. It was paradise for horses. We were well cared for; the hilly paddocks were spacious, and the food was the best. The barns had no stalls and were filled with soft, chest-deep hay."

"How does a Lipizzaner become a performer?"

"A stallion has to show that he wants to learn and likes to play in public."

"Only males perform?"

"Yes."

"Why?"

"I am not sure. It is a tradition. But I would love to perform with mares."

"When does training begin?"

"When a horse is four years old, but riding does not start until the fifth year."

"Why wait so long?"

"All Lipizzaners are treated with great care. Our bodies are allowed to develop without undue stress so that we may live long lives. Plus, a horse has to have the right appearance. Many foals are born a dark color. After several seasons some colts turn white. Only one out of every five Lipizzaner stallions becomes a public performer at the Spanish Riding School."

"What happens to the other horses?"

"They are kept on the farm for breeding or sold to the public. Lipizzaners are great for pleasure riding. We also make terrific harness horses. The people on the farm make sure the prospective owner of a Lipizzaner is qualified."

"They check up on the buyers?"

"Definitely; here horses come first."

"Why is it called the Spanish Riding School?"

"Our blood lines extend back to Spain."

"When did horses start performing?"

"The first public performances were in ancient times when generals reviewed their armies. Soldiers would parade past with a smart step to impress their leaders. The Greek general, Xenophon, taught his horses special gaits for battle and for show. When paraded, their high-stepping action gave the chargers an exceptional look.

"Xenophon recorded his teachings. Those lessons are now referred to as dressage, which means training in French. The Spanish Riding School is the oldest of its kind practicing the ancient arts. And even though some of the maneuvers were created for war, we thankfully now only perform for people's pleasure."

"What is the oldest ongoing public event for horses?"

"It's the Lord Mayor's Show, a festive annual parade in London that began almost eight hundred years ago to celebrate the birth of democracy. The Lord Mayor was the first directly-elected official in England. Each year the new Lord Mayor, whose position was second only to the Queen or King of England, was required to be presented to the people of London.

"The show is the oldest and one of the largest processions in the equine world. Hundreds of horses and thousands of people parade to the music of marching bands. One year it was so popular, the parade was run a second time.

"Even part of the Household Cavalry, highly trained horsemen that lead their horses by reins attached to their ankles or wrists while simultaneously playing musical instruments, participate in the show. But sometimes, mishaps occur. One Lord Mayor stopped for some ale during the parade and accidentally dropped his tankard. His horse, startled by the sound, reared and threw the newly elected Lord Mayor, who unfortunately died. In another parade, a Lord Mayor fell from his horse but fortunately only broke a leg.

"The next Lord Mayor opted for the safety of a horse-drawn carriage, a tradition carried on today. A beautiful, gilded State Coach, used only for the Lord Mayor's Show, is drawn by six magnificent black Shire horses."

"In what other shows do horses perform?"

"Many shows feature horses. A soldier of the United Kingdom's Calvary Dragoons founded the first modern circus. His excellent displays of trick riding, designed to advertise his school of traditional horsemanship, became a thriving circus. Today hundreds of circuses and fairs all over the world use performing horses to entertain people.

"Buffalo Bill's Wild West Show was the first in America. People paid to see horses and people perform a type of theater that demonstrated the early way of life in the American West."

"What is your favorite type of performance?"

"Equines performing at liberty."

"What do you mean?"

"At liberty means performing without direct physical contact. Like the equine ballet at the Bowmanville Zoo near Toronto, created by Mike Hackenberger. The experienced equine troupe consists of Lucas, a giant Belgium; Rusty and Mr. Stubs, two tiny miniatures that could almost walk under Lucas's belly; and Pepsi and Dijor, two zebras from Africa. Playing totally at liberty they maneuver, dance, and spin like ballerinas. The horses really love Mike because he always puts their needs first."

"The way Hans takes care of you?"

"Exactly. We have no pressure during practice—it has to be fun. As trust develops, a close friendship between horse and human ensues. Successful results require that each intimately knows and trusts the other. This takes dedication for which many people in today's world seem to have no time. Patience, understanding, and respect are the main ingredients for a successful partnership. When people put their interests above the horse's needs rather than working as a team, they fail to bond and the horse's performance is less exuberant."

"Does Mr. Riegler train other Lipizzaners?"

"He has trained over fifty performing steeds. Hans has been with the Imperial Spanish Riding School for more than thirty years. He is the school's thirty-third Chief Rider, a post that dates back to 1710. Since their knowledge is only shared orally, Hans has nearly three hundred years of accumulated horsemanship wisdom. He is an exceptional man among men."

"How long does it take to train a performer?"

"A Lipizzaner is a world-class athlete; training takes up to eight years. Individual treatment of each stallion is the absolute essence of the school's philosophy. Training here is not a competition; it is about building trust between individuals. During daily training, it does not matter what is done, but how it is done. The exercises are designed to strengthen a horse and prolong his life."

"How long does it take to train a rider?"

"It takes ten to fifteen years."

"It takes longer to train the man than the horse?"

"Yes. A horse is much more sensitive to his surroundings and environment. It is easier for the ridden to sense whether the rider is balanced. And just like a horse, each rider's personal development is conducted on an individualized schedule. The commitment to the ancient art of horse-man-ship has led to the Imperial Spanish Riding School's worldwide reputation. Even after a person is selected to come to the school, half will drop out before becoming public performers."

"How old are the new students?"

"Fifteen to eighteen years old, but Hans prefers they start at fifteen."

"Do they need to be capable riders when they apply?"

"The prospective student needs to be healthy and athletic but not necessarily experienced with horses. In fact, since many skilled riders have developed bad habits and rely on improper aids that are not used here, prior training might be detrimental to their equine education."

"What is the training like?"

"It is essential that training is conducted without tension to avoid overtaxing the horses. Straightforward riding, with the horse in the most natural position for the walk, trot, and gallop, teaches the rider a balanced seat. Through practice, the student gains a lightness and ease that enables free riding. Then each horse and rider learn many movements. But the public performances have been the same for almost one hundred years."

"Do the steeds know the difference between a practice and a performance?"

"On public performance days, the caregivers come in early and take extra time to groom us. We feel the excitement in the air when spectators fill the hall and the music begins. When we enter the arena, we are at our best. The public performances help fulfill our mission, which is to give people a greater appreciation for the horse-human bond. Our reputation is known internationally, as we have performed around the world."

"If allowed, would you still perform?"

"Yes, I love performing. Hans and I have great fun together. Educational play is the key at the Spanish Riding School. Training and performance are the same—a type of play. Some of the friendships between horses and people here are among the most intimate interspecies relationships in the world. Most people who have watched us perform have a greater appreciation for horses in general. It's the Lipizzaners' way of educating people, to preserve a gentler way of life through mutual respect and cooperation with other species."

"How long does a public performance last?"

"Approximately ninety minutes."

"How many horses participate?"

"Up to eight perform at one time. Each horse has a specialty. At the start of the performance, young stallions show the basic movements of walk, trot, and gallop.

"In doing steps, the horse places his legs diagonally in front of each other so that all four hoof beats are heard. During trotting, the diagonal pair of legs push off and land simultaneously, with two distinctive hoof beats. When we gallop around the perimeter of the arena or in figure eights at our fastest pace, three beats of the hooves can be heard.

"Then mature stallions perform more advanced gaits that include the piaffe, a diagonal movement of the legs with the horse advancing minimally, and the graceful pirouette in which we turn in eight equal leaps around our hocks.

"But the gait the Lipizzaners made famous, nicknamed the "Spanish step," is the passage. The horse alternates from one diagonal pair of legs to the other by pushing off with a springing motion with only a small frontal and upward thrust. Horses around the world practice the passage, but few match the Lipizzaners' advanced technique. With our high leg action, we appear to float between strides."

"Your "Spanish step" this morning looked like an effortless dance."

"Thank you."

"What comes next?"

"The pas de deux is a ballet performed by two pairs. The beautifully choreographed movements are executed in exact mirror image. Next are demonstrations on the short and long rein. This performance requires a particularly well-matched pair. The rider stands on the ground and the stallion displays all steps and figures with only light guidance from the reins. My specialty, the "schools above the ground," comes last."

"Were those the spectacular leaps you made?"

"You liked them?"

"Yes, they were amazing. What do you call the one in which you slowly rose with Hans on your back and remained motionless like a statue?"

"It is called the levade."

"Then you rose and hopped like a kangaroo."

"That is called the courbette, which was originally a military maneuver designed to protect a rider, who was surrounded by enemy infantry. One morning when Hans was teaching me the move by long rein from the ground he slipped and fell underneath me while I was in the air. I landed with one hoof on the ground and the other on Hans' lower leg. I knew if I landed with equal weight that I would have badly broken his leg. So I bore all the weight on my grounded leg and managed to hop again without hurting Hans," said Europa happily.

"What did Hans do?"

"Hans sustained only a small bruise, but was nearly in tears because he thought his slip had cost us both our careers. He could not believe that his leg was not broken, while I risked breaking my own to save him. After that, Hans promised to always take care of me."

"What was the last sensational leap where you jumped more than five feet in the air, and at the highest point, vigorously kicked out your hindquarters? That was incredible!"

"That is our most challenging maneuver, called the capriole."

"Is that how the public performances end?"

"The final movement is called the "school quadrille." It is presented with eight stallions and riders moving as one. We usually receive loud ovations for this, which we greatly appreciate."

"When did the school change from military training to public performing?"

"The shift evolved over hundreds of years. The first public performance was more than three hundred years ago, during the marriage of Emperor Leopold I to Margarita Teresa. More than four hundred horses participated in the wedding celebration. One particular performance involved the rosseballett, or horse ballet, in which the horses danced to musical accompaniment. The new Empress loved the horse show, and during her reign, staged riding games, tournaments, magnificent court balls, and ladies' carousels."

"What was the ladies' carousel?"

"It combined competition and theater, which included men, women, and horses."

"What other uses has the school had?"

"The riding school's main purpose was to develop the mental communication and physical ability between horse and man to perfection. Besides training military officers, royalty and nobility were educated here, because when a man of high social stature rode a horse in public, it was vital that he control his mount. The horses relished the change from combat to presentation even though it evolved slowly."

"If you were not a performing Lipizzaner, what would you prefer to do?"

"I would choose to be a sporting horse, because I like games of skill, but more importantly I would like to have had the opportunity to perform with women."

"Why are there no women riders here?"

"The school has a military history that precludes women. This is the school's only drawback. Don't get me wrong, I love it here and feel incredibly lucky to be partnered with Hans. He is one man who has a genuine appreciation for interspecies relationships."

"Where might I meet a sporting horse?"

"You should meet my cousin Indy, who lives in England, and was once a national cross-country champion."

*"A horse can make you feel like you are capable
of doing anything, even if you're not a master rider,
or even a talented rider."*

- REBECCA BAYOT

Sporting Horses

Indy; Somerset, England

Philippa "Pip" Unwin, Indy's owner, invited me to meet her horses and met me at the Somerset train station. With her was Wendy, an aroma therapist from Manchester, who had come to work with Pip's horses.

Pip drove Wendy and I to our rooms at The Fitzhead Inn, an ivy covered 350-year-old tavern. An outside stairway in the courtyard was lined with old knee-high rubber boots overflowing with flowers. Ducks in the yard welcomed our arrival.

The cozy pub was adorned with equine drawings. One depicted riders in crimson coats gathered with their horses in front of the inn. Another showed men restraining an eager pack of hounds. In the third, a fox, attempting to escape the detection of its pursuers, was darting under a hedgerow. My favorite drawing was from a rider's perspective, and depicted a horse's ears and poll in the foreground, with beautiful, unspoiled country extending to the horizon. Below the picture was written, "The best view in Europe."

My remodeled room across the yard had originally been a stable, which dated back more than four hundred years—a great place for happy horse dreams.

The next morning, Wendy and I drove along a road lined with encroaching hedgerows. Hilly pastures surrounded Pip's stables. By the time we arrived, Pip had gathered four horses from the field. Contentedly looking out from their stalls were Indy, Prince, Mica, and Ash.

Beautiful, healthy thirteen-year-old Indy stood over fourteen hands high. His body was dark brown, and his mane and tail were black. He had white socks on three of his muscular legs and a short, pointed white stripe on the tip of his nose. He was friendly and intelligent.

Pip introduced me to Indy, then left us alone. She and Wendy went to work with Prince, a gentle, giant draft, who towered over the women.

Indy animatedly asked me to brush him down. I asked permission from Pip, who gladly supplied me with the equipment. While grooming Indy, I asked him what he thought of Pip.

"She is the best person I have ever met. I have had other owners, but none were as kind or caring. Pip allows a horse to be a horse. When she was a youngster, Pip took many equine classes, in which the male instructors stressed the importance of domination over horses, which frustrated her.

"Instead, Pip developed her own way of harmonious horsemanship. Pip is open and honest. She set my spirit free and became my best friend. I developed confidence and trust in her leadership. When Pip is working with me, I can read her thoughts. She is also a Reiki Master and practices the art on horses as well as people."

"What is Reiki?"

"It is a technique that helps channel universal life energy."

"How do you benefit from Reiki?"

"I love the attention, and Reiki induced healing. Pip is very compassionate. She is incredibly patient and likes to use play as lessons for learning. She is a leader that any horse would want as a partner. Our health is most important, so she hires many medical professionals to give us therapy."

"How does aroma therapy work?"

"Wendy's silver box has numerous bottles of oil, each of which has a unique benefit. Horses select the ones they need. First, Wendy presents an open bottle of oil to a horse. The horse will then signify whether it needs that particular oil by licking its lips and nodding its head, or by turning away."

"How do horses know?"

"Oils tend to have bitter aromas, but the smell becomes sweet when we have a particular need. In the wild, horses routinely self-medicate with plants. But in domestic situations, our diets are usually controlled, so access to medicinal plants is limited."

"How do oils help you?"

"Oils have different properties. For example, linden oil helps with anxiety, whereas marigold oil promotes general healing."

"How is the oil dispensed?"

"Being a true professional, Wendy puts a few drops on Pip's palm, and the horse licks it off. She has the caregiver supply the oil, which promotes bonding between horse and human."

"What else makes Pip exceptional?"

"Pip is patient; the most important quality. Ash and Mica are good examples. Ash came here injured several months ago, but has not been worked even once. Pip will wait until Ash is ready. Pretty Mica, a prized show jumper, was also severely injured, but now plays regularly and is almost ready to be ridden again. Most owners would have destroyed these horses. And let me tell you, Ash and Mica will not forget Pip and will give all their effort for her."

"Have you and Pip competed together?"

"We won a sixty mile endurance race—without finishing first! I was delighted to be in the lead for most of the race, but we were overtaken near the end. I wanted to surge back into the lead, but knowing that I was tiring fast, Pip would not let me.

So we finished second. During the checkup after the race, the first horse came up lame and was penalized. By caring for my health first, we became National Novice Cross-Country Champions!" Indy happily shook his head and kicked the stall wall. Pip looked up and smiled. Indy whinnied gleefully, making Pip laugh.

"Is there much supervision in long distance races?"

"In the past, winning was the main focus; not the horse's health. Endurance racing could be unusually cruel and could last for days. Usually, horses were ridden from sunup to sundown. One brutal race was run from central Iran to Moscow, Russia, a distance of almost three thousand miles, which included trekking through an arid desert. Most of the horses perished. The eventual winner, Turkoman, took eighty-four days to finish.

"Equines living in the wild would never run so fast for so long. Many horses in endurance racing die young, because they are pushed too hard."

"Is this true for all equine sports?"

"Yes, for most. It is strange to us that play can cause some people to act in irrational ways, which exposes us to injury and death. Some people will do almost anything to win a competition. Many men view the horse as a commodity, rather than as a fellow sentient being.

"An exception is the Mongolian horsemen. The Mongolians are a proud people, who take great care in raising and training horses. If a horse founders during a long race, the owner, who is also the trainer, feels disgraced.

"In the American West, Frank Hopkins was a great long-distance racer. His awareness of the horses' health enabled him to have a prolific winning record. To horses, he was like a brother. Just like Linda Tellington-Jones is our sister. Linda, a great endurance champion, competes against both men and women and always puts the health of her horses first."

"Do horses in the wild compete?"

"Equines continually play brief games to strengthen themselves and to establish their standing within the family. Horses compete to be faster and stronger, but they immediately break off engagements that might endanger their health. Horses in the wild help all the members of their family survive. A dispute ending in a horse's lameness weakens everyone.

"Human competitions usually last longer and are much more stressful. As a rule, a horse cannot choose to quit a human's game, so horses can easily be prodded and pushed until they are injured."

"When did people start playing with horses?"

"Thousands of years ago, head to head racing was the first sport that included horses. Team sports also extend back several millennia to when people in the Far East played a game called "tchigan," an extremely dangerous form of tennis on horseback, which evolved into the game of equestrian polo. In the ancient Olympics, horses first pulled chariots, then a century later, were ridden in races."

"Did women compete in the early Olympics?"

"Unfortunately, women were not allowed to compete or even to watch the Games. Nor were they allowed to play polo when it was first brought to the West."

Indy paused for a long moment, then explained, "Men subjugated women by not letting them compete in equine sports, purportedly for their own safety. They never mentioned the fact that men were also frequently injured in competition. Men argued that women should be docile followers rather than leaders. In reality, men knew that women on horses would be their equal. Some men were threatened by the possibility that a woman might win the competition.

"Thousands of years ago, before our domestication across cultures worldwide, man developed the need to dominate the female of his species. We don't know how paternal societies originated. We just know that the relationship between men and women became unbalanced, which endangered all species."

"How do you know this?"

"Horses are great observers. We recognize unhealthy relationships and have been worried about man's need to dominate women for many generations. We remember sidesaddles being used to put women at a disadvantage. Using a sidesaddle was not an efficient way to ride or talk with your body to a horse. Thankfully, women can now compete equally in many equine sports."

"Are equine games safer today?"

"Definitely. We are thankful that numerous governing bodies now exist for many equine competitions, and regulations provide for the horses' health. Most marathon contests are now closely supervised, with several veterinary checkpoints. A veterinarian may retire a competitor at any time a horse shows potential lameness. Unfortunately, some people still press their horses beyond safe humane limits."

"Do horses like playing people's games?"

"Remember, every horse is a unique individual. Some like to play to please their caregiver, others like competition, and some don't like human games at all. So people need to take their time and carefully observe each horse to ensure that he or she is a willing competitor."

"What is your least favorite human sport?"

"Bullfighting!" exclaimed Indy with a roar. "The bull doesn't stand a chance, and even though we are heavily padded, an enraged bull might gore a horse."

"How do horses partake in bullfighting?"

"At the start, mounted men, or picadors, repeatedly swoop in and stab the bull in its neck and shoulders with lances, severing those muscles. The bull then cannot lift its head to defend itself properly, which makes it easier for the matador to kill him. Horses never have enjoyed hunting or any sport that involves the murder of another animal."

"What sports do horses like?"

"Many western riding competitions and rodeos, given the way they are now regulated, can be fun for horses. We like to compete in barrel racing, cutting, reining, and saddle or bareback bucking contests."

"Which rodeo event is your favorite?"

"Bareback bucking," exclaimed Indy, as he joyfully kicked out his back legs.

"Why?" I asked in wide-eyed awe of his powerful display.

"It's our chance, without blame or punishment, to get a little payback for all the indecencies man has committed against us. Bucking horses take great pride in unseating a man and loosening the irritable girth strap in less than eight seconds; the required length of time a cowboy has to stay on a horse to score points."

"Who was the greatest bucking horse?"

"There are many great bucking broncos, but Necktie and the giant, General Pershing, were especially intimidating. Few cowboys stayed on for the required time, and many walked away nursing bumps and bruises," nickered Indy.

"Why do horses enjoy reining?"

"It is fun, because the rider with the softest hands, which makes the bit easier on our mouth, usually wins. Reining requires a horse to perform circles, spins, and sudden skidding stops at top speed, with as few visible cues from the rider as possible."

"And why do horses like cutting contests?"

"Cutting is an event in which the horse and rider separate, or cut out, a particular cow from a herd. Cutting is gratifying, because in order to win, the cowboy must speak with his eyes and mind, giving control to the horse. The horse's cagey, side to side, fast-paced maneuvers separate the cow from the herd. A good cowboy lets the horse take the lead, tries to maintain his balance, and enjoys the ride."

"Who was the best rodeo cowboy?"

"We loved the Dorrance brothers and Ray Hunt. They were always kind to horses and truly loved us. They were excellent observers of a horse's body language, took their time training, and put our health first. They professed and practiced a soft, gentle approach of connected companionship. Monty Roberts is another cowboy we admire, because he is also against the domineering methods practiced by many male horse trainers. There would be fewer problems in the world if people practiced more kindness, respect, sensitivity, and patience in all their relationships."

"Why do horses like barrel racing?"

"Because it involves women riders and is a short sprint. Horses also enjoy pole bending, flag and keyhole racing, tent pegging, and other short sprint games, known as Gymkhana, because they involve children."

"What rodeo sport would you like to play?"

"I would like to be part of the pickup team, the unsung heroes of the rodeo. They do not compete, but are there for the contestants' safety. A pickup team member has to be able to ride and rope skillfully. The horse needs to be athletic and not shy away from danger. For example, at the end of a successful bronco ride, the pickup team races in and helps the cowboy off the bucking horse. It would be impossible to run a rodeo without the help of pickup people on horseback."

"What is the horses' least favorite rodeo event?"

"The wild horse and wagon races, because the horses involved have had little or no experience with people and are subjected to harsh treatment. The wild steeds are forcibly bridled, with the bit jammed into their mouths, and saddled or harnessed, then are ridden or driven. As a result, many frightened horses have become injured, and some have died. Fortunately, there are few wild horse races left, and one day we hope the evil event will be stopped."

"How were rodeo competitions created?"

"Over one hundred years ago, cowboys from different ranches created games to test their working skills. Now there are hundreds of sanctioned western riding competitions and rodeos each year. There is also a professional women's rodeo circuit in which many horses enjoy participating."

"Have other sports sprung from work-related activities?"

"Many sports were created to prepare horses for war. During the Middle Ages, all over Europe, tournaments became the favorite form of recreation for knights, and the joust was the most popular event. It involved two heavily armored horses and riders. The riders carried a long lance and a shield and charged at one another with the intention of unseating their opponent. Hundreds of years ago, the contest was fought using a blunt lance for a safe competition or a pointed lance that could result in serious injury or death. Jousting, using a blunt lance, is still the official sport in the state of Maryland."

"What other sports do horses enjoy today?"

"Vaulting, dressage, cross-country, and show jumping have many levels of involvement that culminate in Grand Prix events and the modern-day Olympics.

"Vaulting involves a horse cantering or trotting in a circle as people perform a variety of gymnastic mounting and dismounting maneuvers. Vaulting requires that a horse maintain a steady pace to make performing safer for the rider.

"Dressage is classical horsemanship, which originated in military training. Students begin with simple exercises that include practicing figure eight patterns, circles, and lateral movements. As riders gain experience, they learn to speak with the horse through the subtle use of movement and shifts in weight, thereby acquiring a balanced seat. An experienced, in-tune rider will sense the harmony and willingness from a horse. Dressage is a discipline that can tighten the bond between a horse and a human. But care needs to be taken to insure that the horse is not subjected to too much stress by repetitive practice.

"From local and regional competitions, horses and riders could progress all the way to the Olympics. Though until recently, only military personnel could compete in equine events at the Games, which formerly excluded women."

"What about jumping competitions?"

"There are two basic classifications: hunter-jumpers and jumpers. Hunter-jumpers are judged on pace, style, and manner; whereas jumpers compete solely against the clock and the number of faults they commit. Refusing to jump, or knocking down part of a barrier, are faults, which result in a time penalty."

"Please describe the cross-country competitions."

"A cross-country race, run on varying terrain, incorporates uphill and downhill jumps over manmade and natural obstacles. Run against the clock, it can be rigorous and demanding, plus penalty time is added for falling or refusing jumps.

"The triathlon of equestrian riding, called "eventing," can be extremely challenging. The events include dressage, cross-country riding, and show jumping."

"Why do you like the modern Olympics?"

"We love to see women competing with men in the equestrian events. That inclusion is very uplifting for women and equines."

"Has a female rider ever won an Olympic medal?"

"In 1952, when women and men competed head to head for the first time, Denmark's Liz Hartel, riding Jubilee, won the silver medal in dressage. The accomplishment of her second place finish in competition with men was intensified, because Liz also had to deal with the physical effects of polio. It was a defining moment for horses and women," stated Indy proudly. "Liz and Jubilee proved that their skill was no fluke, for they won the silver medal a second time in the following Olympics."

"Liz Hartel was physically handicapped?"

"Horses really dislike the word, handicapped, and the way people usually treat those who are physically or mentally challenged. We believe that every person has different abilities and should be treated with respect and appreciation for their unique qualities. That is the equine way."

"Did Liz and Jubilee change the equine sporting world?"

"That pair inspired a generation of females. Subsequently, women's participation greatly increased in most equine sports. This, in turn, reinforced horses' resolve to empower women. Today, nearly four out of five people involved in equine recreation and sports are female.

"We still willingly participate in the Olympics even though cross-country courses and stadium jumping are continually being made more challenging, which unfortunately increases the risk of injury or death for horses and, sometimes, people. Do you remember Christopher Reeve, the actor? He was a kind man, who was critically injured in a lower-level equestrian event. The risk of injury is inherent in all equine sports—even Olympic riders have been injured, a few mortally," stated Indy sadly.

"What caused Mr. Reeve's accident?"

"Most people didn't know that before the event, his horse had been overworked for several days and was tired. The horse shied away from a combination jump at the last moment. Christopher was thrown, landed on his head, and was regrettably paralyzed."

"Would you change any equestrian rules?"

"Horses would love to have all equestrian events be bit-less. That would truly create competitions in which the best rider wins. Plus, the courses could be less demanding, decreasing the risks to both horse and rider, while ultimately increasing the level of challenge."

"Are there other contests horses enjoy?"

"Although each horse has individual preferences, we like many driving and show competitions in which we pull carriages, carts, or wagons; we especially like working in pairs. When we are paired for driving, we have another horse beside us for companionship and load-sharing. Plus, pulling a load can be easier on a horse than carrying a rider—especially an unbalanced one. Driving also allows people, who might not be able to ride, to enjoy equestrian endeavors."

"What is the most unusual sport that horses enjoy?"

"I think that would be skijoring," stated Indy with a happy snort. "Skijoring is a sport run on snow. A sprinting horse and rider tow a person on skis clutching a rope through a slalom course and over jumps. There is little stress for horses because the sport is run on snow and is more for fun than competition. Plus, the horses run in a quick, short spurt, which is how horses like to play in the wild."

"What are some recreations that horses enjoy?"

"Most horses enjoy trail rides. Plus, many would like to be in a pony club to educate and play with children."

"Do horses like show competitions?"

"Yes, horse shows can be fun and a valuable learning experience. The groundwork required between horse and human promotes bonding, though people's urge to win sometimes causes them to act in cruel ways by docking a horse's tail or trimming our whiskers."

"What is docking?"

"It's the shearing of a horse's tail for the sake of appearance. Our tail is very important to us, for communication and as a fly swatter. Thankfully, docking is now considered cruel and is an uncommon practice."

"How does whisker trimming affect a horse?"

"We use whiskers as feelers to move through narrow spaces and the dark, so we don't crash into things. One of our two blind spots is at the tip of the nose, so our whiskers help us to judge up-close distances."

"Indy, what is your favorite sport?"

"I just love to play with Pip."

"What do you mean by play?"

"Equines like to recreate with people without the pressure of competition. Play can take numerous forms and may be entertaining, fun, and liberating. Play is a learning experience that stimulates bonding. Fun for horses may be as simple as going for a walk, exercising side by side, or being ridden for the joy of companionship. Just watch Pip play with Mica and Prince."

Pip led the horses, both at liberty, to the center of the indoor arena. They waited patiently while Pip turned on some upbeat Latin music and retrieved a giant three-foot diameter rubber ball.

"What is Pip doing with the ball?"

"She wants to exercise and play with the horses while she examines them. Pip will slowly bounce the ball to attract their attention. When she turns toward Prince and Mica, they will slowly walk around the perimeter of the arena in time to the ball's bounce. When Pip bounces the ball faster, both horses will match the ball's pace with a canter, then a trot. This is done at complete liberty. Prince and Mica have the freedom to respond as they choose. They like to play, but they could decide not to participate."

When the ball stopped bouncing, Prince and Mica came to a halt. When Pip rolled the ball away, the horses remained motionless.

"What is Pip doing now?"

"Pip wants the horses to focus their attention on her, not the ball. When Pip walks to the center of the arena, Prince and Mica will follow and match their front left-right leg movements with hers. When Pip trots, the horses mirror her gait. When she turns, they turn. Pip never says a word; she communicates visually, and all the while she is observing the quality of the horses' strides, body language, and breathing. By the position of their upright ears, she knows that the horses are enjoying themselves.

"Now watch. Do you see? Pip has come to a stop—she has seen a break in Mica's gait. Prince has moved aside, on his own, to let them work together."

"What is wrong?"

"Before coming here, Mica landed hard after a jump and cracked a cannon bone. Although Mica likes to play, Pip wants to make sure that Mica is not pushing herself too hard, and that she doesn't accidentally get re-injured. Now, Mica has persuaded Pip that she wants to carry on."

Pip and Mica played by walking, trotting, and cantering around the arena, as Prince calmly waited.

"Will Pip ride Prince or Mica today?"

"They are not ready yet, but their training is increasing their stamina. She will play with each individually while concentrating on the horse's health and ability."

As Pip finished up and started toward us, Indy excitedly began shifting his weight from leg to leg to warm up for their play session. He was obviously anxious to display his talents, and continued, "Pip and I are closely bonded. All we need is a soft riding pad and a halter with reins, but no bit, saddle, or stirrups," stated Indy proudly.

I watched as Pip and Indy performed maneuvers—walking, trotting, and cantering around the arena. Two had become one, and Indy's happy snorts clearly indicated his pleasure. All too soon, they finished, and I gave them a standing ovation.

Pip wanted Indy to cool down before feeding him, so she and Wendy went to tend the other horses and asked me to brush him down. I was smiling from ear to ear while grooming Indy, and I thanked him for the wonderful display.

"You're welcome. It was just play between good friends," answered Indy as he fondly gazed over his shoulder at Pip. "For me, Pip makes up for all the injustices done to horses and gives me hope for the future. We need many more females like Pip. Horses empowering women will help save the Earth."

I asked Indy what he would like to do after his competition days were over.

Indy whinnied affectionately as Pip returned with his meal. Before he began munching, Indy said, "Some horses enlighten many people at once by becoming equine actors. I would like to try that role. You should visit an equine actor in Hollywood to learn their story."

*"There is something about riding down the street
on a prancing horse that makes you feel like something,
even when you ain't a thing."*

- WILL ROGERS

HOLLYWOOD HORSES

Beechnut; Malibu, California

I n the private library of the Gene Autry Museum in California, I learned that several equine actors lived at Will Rogers State Park, located by the ocean near Hollywood. At the park the smell of the sea hung in the air, and tall broad-leafed trees amply shaded the stables.

Horses were being tacked up as a group prepared to tour the park; property that was once Will Rogers' private ranch. In the adjacent outdoor paddock, a woman was taking a riding lesson. The indoor arena was quiet and cool. Photographs of a smiling Mr. Rogers and friends on horseback, posing near the stables, adorned the walls. The park still retained the idyllic feeling evident in the pictures from the past.

When an employee approached, I inquired about the equine actors presently living there. She invited me to meet Beechnut.

He caught my eye immediately. Beechnut was very handsome. His body, mane, and tail were black; a white hourglass figure decorated his face. He introduced himself and asked, "May I help you?"

I told him my mission and asked whether he had performed in movies.

"I have acted in films and know all about the motion picture industry."

I smiled, reached out my hand, palm down, and waited until he checked me out. After he gave me a nod of approval, I lightly rubbed his nose, massaged his neck, and asked, "What was your biggest acting role?"

"Have you seen *City Slickers?*"

"Yes, which part did you play?"

"The horse for the main character, Billy Crystal," Beechnut stated proudly.

"Did you like Mr. Crystal?"

"Yes, Billy is a great person; we are good friends. He liked me so much he purchased me after the film was finished. Billy told me never to worry, because he would always take care of me."

"How old are you?"

"I am twenty-three."

"Wow, you look great."

"Thanks, the people here are kind, and we are well cared for."

"That's wonderful. Could you explain how horses became movie stars?"

"At the beginning of the Industrial Revolution, horses still played vital roles for people. As more motorized machinery was invented, large numbers of horses were put out of work. At first, we were thankful to be relieved of our burdens and hoped our dreams of living with people in enjoyable domestic bliss had come true. Instead, we were shocked as millions of our siblings were slaughtered for fertilizer or pet food. Our numbers shrank drastically, as did our influence in people's everyday lives. Starring in movies has provided horses with an opportunity to reach out and touch many people's souls."

"When did horses first appear on film?"

"Before the movie camera was invented."

"I don't understand."

"Around a hundred years ago, people still debated whether a horse's hooves simultaneously left the ground when galloping. A prominent person wanted to settle the dispute. He hired a large crew of people, set up a row of still cameras close together, and took pictures in rapid succession. These photographs, when viewed quickly in sequence, gave the impression of a body in motion and ultimately proved what we already knew: that indeed a horse's hooves all leave the ground at the same time when running."

"When did horses initially appear in movies?"

"Motion pictures in America were started by the inventor Thomas Edison. His first film lasted less than thirty seconds and was called *Bucking Bronco*. The film starred Sunfish, who bucked a man around an arena."

"What was the first feature film?"

"*The Great Train Robbery*. That picture was actually shot in New Jersey and included horses."

"When did they start shooting in Hollywood?"

"Shortly after that first film was made, when almost all movies included horses. In some films, we played heroic roles. One popular silent feature was titled *Saved by Her Horse,* which was followed by *Saved by His Horse*.

"Horses have appeared and starred in more movies than any other animal. Studios have made many racehorse and horse race films. And it would be almost impossible to have a cowboy in a Western and not include his horse. Thousands of equine extras have hauled wagons and carried cavalry in war sagas. In the film, *Cimarron*, more than a thousand chargers were used; their powerful performance helped the movie win the Oscar for Best Picture."

"Who were the first Hollywood horse heroes?"

"Silver King, a beautiful white stallion, worked with silent film star, Fred Thompson. The horse had a great personality and acting ability, which enhanced many of his stunts and tricks. Fred loved Silver King, bought the equine star, and built a luxurious stable adjacent to his home for his friend.

"Another horse hero was the red and white pinto, Fritz, who was also loved by his partner, co-actor, and owner, William Hart. They appeared in many silent movies together. Another star was Beverly, a mare who rescued Marilyn Mills in *The Rip Snorter* and *Trick*. And in *My Pal*, Star saved the day by untying the lead actor.

"The first equine superstar in Hollywood was Tony, the Wonder Horse, Tom Mix's famous charger. When Tom was a horse handler, he spotted Tony and purchased him. They became best friends and could read each other's thoughts. Performing their own stunts, Tom and Tony starred in many profitable movies.

"Tony was the first horse to get his hoof prints on the Hollywood Walk of Fame. Unfortunately, a few years later while filming, Tony accidentally stumbled during a chase scene and rolled over Tom. Both actors were seriously injured, and Tony had to retire."

"Do horses have a favorite actor?"

"Will Rogers, a gentle Cherokee Indian, a cowboy, and one of the best ropers in the world before he started acting, worked with many horses. He was a rare man that every equine wished to have as a friend. Will loved life and respected men, women, horses, and all animals. It was a very sad day when he died in a plane crash. He was a ray of hope among men in Hollywood, because he took umbrage with the way equine actors were treated during filming."

"Were horses harmed while making movies?"

"Early movie-making was hard on many horses. Numerous equine actors were paired with men who treated them cruelly, and only a few women were given the opportunity to act with horses. Hundreds of horses perished making movies, because to get the best action shots, directors gave little regard to a horse's health. Animal actors were frequently treated like props. Cruel hobbles were used on horses to achieve dramatic effects.

"One particularly inhumane technique was used to make a horse fall on cue. The procedure involved wrapping burly leather straps around a horse's front legs. A thin, strong wire was tied to the leather bands. The other end of the wire, which was more than a hundred feet long, was firmly anchored to the ground. The long length of wire allowed a horse to gallop at full speed before becoming taut, which caused the sprinting horse to take a hard, headfirst tumble. Another cruel approach for making a horse fall, at a precise point, was to dig a shallow pit and camouflage it. The unknowing steed running into it would fall hard and somersault forward head over hooves. Countless horses were hurt and many died due to injuries sustained for a particular cinematic effect.

"Some horses were literally pushed off high cliffs, and others were raced to death, for theatrical purposes. Have you seen the movie, *Ben Hur*?"

"In which Charlton Heston drove beautiful white horses in an amazing race?"

"That was the second *Ben Hur* movie, after the American Humane Association (AHA) came to our rescue. The original *Ben Hur* was a silent film. During its making, scores of horses died, and many others received crippling injuries. It was a horrifying display of disregard for life."

"When did the association become involved in the motion picture industry?"

"After completing *The Charge of the Light Brigade* in the 1940s, in which more than fifty horses were cruelly tripped in just one scene, and also, in response to the deaths of horses during the filming of *Jesse James*.

"Currently the AHA protects all animal actors from harm and mistreatment."

"How is the AHA administered?"

"It is staffed primarily by women and funded by grants and public donations. The personnel, routinely present on film sets, supervise the care and handling of the animal actors. Horses are extremely grateful for their presence.

"The AHA has affected movie-making in several other positive ways. To receive AHA endorsement, no animal is allowed to be injured or killed during filming. The AHA established guidelines for the safe use of all animal actors. Making movies with animals, especially horses, is a big production. Trainers, handlers, and veterinarians have to be employed.

"There are also rules that stunt horses be trained specifically for falling, leaping, and rearing. To ensure a horse's safety, a jump may not be made from a height of more than six feet, and the landing must be well padded. The rest of a thrilling fall is left up to the special effects technicians.

"The regulations also require that when rearing horses are used for fight scenes, the horses' hooves are wrapped in rubber, and a special non-pulling tape is used on their mouths to prevent accidental biting.

"Great care is now taken for our safety while performing. For example, in a stunt in which a runaway stagecoach or wagon tips over, the horses are automatically released from the carriage just before it rolls. Or when a scene calls for a horse to kick out a wooden wall or door, it is made of soft, scored balsa wood that splinters with little effort.

"The involvement of the AHA also led directors to seek horses that could perform unique acts, which enabled those steeds to become celebrities. Horse doubles are often employed to perform stunts to protect the equine star."

"Who are some horses that had stand-ins?"

"The handsome chestnut stallion, Champion, once titled The World's Wonder Horse, was the costar of Gene Autry, the singing cowboy. Champion had more than thirty doubles. One horse was used just for publicity photographs, another performed dismounting tricks, and several look-alikes were ridden in the movies and television. With a bit of make-up, Old Baldy, Tennessee, Champ Junior, Little Champ, and Wag all had a chance to play the equine superstar.

"At the height of his career, Champion received more than two hundred fan letters a day. His admiring public loved Champion's unique six-gun bit; two highly polished metal halves of a six-shooter, molded from a toy gun, which was designed by Mr. Autry."

"Which costarring human and horse had the closest bond on film?"

"There have been many great acting teams. One of the best was Roy Rogers and Trigger. Roy was an excellent horseman and could rear on Trigger without any tack. Plus Trigger could walk more than a hundred feet upright on his hind legs and could perform more than fifty other stunts.

"Roy first spotted the beautiful palomino when he was called Golden Cloud, who carried Olivia de Haviland in *The Adventures of Robin Hood*. After Roy bought Trigger, they teamed with Dale Evans and Buttermilk to make the two prettiest pairs in Hollywood. Trigger and Buttermilk received thousands of letters from fans. Roy knew that half the moviegoers really came to see Trigger. After appearing in several films with Roy, Trigger was proclaimed by the media as the smartest horse in Hollywood. Roy and Trigger's film producers made both actors use doubles for their more dangerous stunts. For special public performances, Roy adorned Trigger with expensive tack that gave the equine actor a princely appearance. Trigger's bridle and saddle contained fourteen hundred ounces of silver, more than one hundred ounces of gold, and fifteen hundred rubies!"

"Who are some other famous acting duos?"

"There are too many actors to mention all those who depended on their horses as co-stars, but a few include the Lone Ranger and Silver, Tonto and Scout, and Hopalong Cassidy and Topper. Phantom and Tornado were both paired with Zorro. And while Banner, Duke, Handsome Boy, Dollar, Cochise, and Midnight were lesser-known equine stars, John Wayne and Clint Eastwood would hardly be the superstar cowboy actors they became without the aid of their trusted and intelligent friends."

"Did the actors have a favorite horse?"

"Just like horses, humans are individuals and have distinct preferences and tastes. But the handsome, chestnut-colored Steel, who had a white-blazed face, worked with more leading men than any other horse. Randolph Scott, Clark Gable, Gregory Peck, John Wayne, and Gary Cooper are but a few of the stars who have appeared in movies with Steel."

"Do horses have a favorite film?"

"We have been in too many movies to have a single favorite. But one of the most important for women was *National Velvet*, which starred Elizabeth Taylor as Velvet Brown, and the Thoroughbred, King Charles, as The Pie."

"Why was *National Velvet* so significant?"

"It was the first major film using horses to be adapted from a book written by a woman. Enid Bagnold loved horses and wrote several books about us. The screenplay was also written by a woman, Helen Deutsch, who wanted to make the hopeful messages in the book shine on film."

"What were the messages?"

"The authors wanted to help females to believe in themselves, to trust their equine partners, to have hope, and to persevere in the face of adversity."

"How were those points conveyed?"

"By breaking barriers. In the story, Velvet Brown was a girl who fell in love with her neighbor's beautiful, but unruly, horse, The Pie. The steed was a natural jumper, and on several occasions, left his pasture by easily leaping the large surrounding stone wall. The frustrated owner organized a lottery to rid himself of the horse nobody wanted to buy, and lucky Velvet won.

"Velvet spent most of her free time riding The Pie. They developed a close friendship while galloping across fields and over fences. The Pie was such a great jumper that Velvet wanted to run the Thoroughbred in the biggest race in the country, the Grand National steeplechase. With the help of a friend, Velvet trained the horse but could not find the right jockey. Velvet decided to ride The Pie by disguising herself as a man. The grueling jumps caused many horses to shy away from the hedges and others to fall, but in an exciting finish, The Pie, a hundred to one shot, won the race.

"Even though they were disqualified, because Velvet was a girl, the message of the movie inspired a generation of female fans to strive for their own personal goals. Velvet and The Pie proved to moviegoers that a woman could ride a horse equally well or even better than a man."

"Did Ms. Taylor and King Charles have a close connection in real life?"

"Actually, Elizabeth Taylor, who was just twelve years old when the movie was made, discovered King Charles, a grandson of the great racehorse Man-of-War, while she was training for the movie. Elizabeth and King Charles had already formed a trusting friendship before filming began.

"Ms. Taylor convinced the producers to cast King Charles as The Pie. The movie was such a great success that they arranged to have King Charles, who was privately owned, to be presented to Elizabeth as a gift. *National Velvet* and King Charles helped propel Elizabeth Taylor's superstar career. Ms. Taylor loved King Charles, and he loved her, because she always treated him like royalty.

"Horses long to have a kind, caring humane partner—a companion who is a sensitive, trustworthy friend and guide. We often find that connection with women. Some men view horses as something to control or dominate, rather than as a partner.

"Sympathetic relationships between species are needed to insure that humans experience the interconnectedness of all life, thus becoming responsible caregivers for our planet. Horses hope to reach out to women, so that together, we can influence and educate people to interact cooperatively and to personally become more kind, caring, nurturing, and compassionate."

"What other books featuring horses and humans were made into movies?"

"*Black Beauty* is the story of a mare's roller coaster ride through life. She was born, in the late eighteen hundreds, into a loving family—a domestic horse heaven—but over the years, circumstances placed her in the hands of several masters, some of whom were quite cruel, until she was finally reunited with her original owners and regained her tranquil life.

"Anna Sewell, the author of *Black Beauty*, was crippled early in life. She enjoyed riding in horse-drawn carriages through which she learned to live in the present, connect with horses, and hear their tales.

"Marguerite Henry is another writer we love. She wrote several equine stories including *King of the Wind* and *Stormy: Misty's Foal*, but *Misty of Chincoteague*, her most famous, was made into a movie."

"Please, tell me the tale."

"It is another inspiring and true story about empowering girls. Misty was a wild pony that lived with her mother, Phantom, in a herd on Assateague Island. The ponies had resided on the otherwise uninhabited land for generations. Once a year, a pony penning day took place; all the horses were driven off the island, and some were captured to be auctioned to the public. This annual event continues to this day and attracts thousands of people."

"Who organizes this, and why?"

"The size of the Assateague herd must be regulated, because the small island is sparsely vegetated and can only support a limited number of horses. The local fire department coordinates the auction as a fundraiser and monitors the owners to ensure the horses' good care."

"How is the movie empowering for girls?"

"Siblings Maureen and Paul fell in love with Phantom and Misty and were lucky enough to acquire them both. Maureen and Paul rode and trained the fast Phantom with equal proficiency and wanted to enter her in the big local race. Because Maureen was just as qualified as her brother to tame the ponies with tenderness and positive reinforcement, the story empowers other girls to train and manage horses. Maureen finally convinces her brother to forego the race and allow Phantom and Misty to return to the herd, because truly loving someone sometimes means you have to let them go."

"What other inspiring roles do horses enjoy playing in the movies?"

"*The Black Stallion*, by Walter Farley, *The Red Pony*, by John Steinbeck, and *My Friend Flicka*, by Mary O'Hara, are all excellent novels made into inspirational films. Plus, some real-life equine stories have been made into movies, including numerous racehorse biographies and tales about races, such as the Kentucky Derby. My favorite is Seabiscuit's story, based on a book written by Laura Hillenbrand. The original film version starred Shirley Temple, a lifelong lover of horses. The remake is a more accurate account of the thoroughbred's life.

"But what is most important to horses is that Seabicuit is remembered. Although he did not have the conformation of a champion, his championship heart was allowed to shine through because of his kind and caring owners, trainer, and jockey, all of whom loved and supported him, had faith in his ability, and recognized his indomitable spirit."

"Did horses have an influence in television?"

"Gene Autry created a television show, without himself, that starred Champion. Also, Roy Rogers and Trigger switched from the large to the small screen. Bonanza, Rawhide, Little House on the Prairie, and every other Western television series needed horses."

"Do you have a favorite equine show?"

"I have always loved the concept of the talking and talented golden palomino, Mr. Ed," stated Beechnut with a broad smile.

"I loved that show, too. How did they make his lips move?"

"Les Hilton, a great equine trainer in Hollywood, developed that trick. Mr. Ed was Les's star pupil, and they were great friends. For several years, they worked very closely together on many stunts and tricks. The lip movement was accomplished with the aid of a thin transparent fishing line. It was threaded from Les's hands, through Ed's halter, and under his top lip. Les, standing just out of the camera's range, slightly tugged the fishing line whenever Mr. Ed spoke aloud.

"Mr. Ed was also very talented and had impeccable timing. He could open and close doors, pick up a telephone receiver, or pull an electrical plug from the wall. Plus he could hold many objects in his mouth, including hats and a large pencil with which to write. Mr. Ed even won the Patsy Award. The award was presented annually for an outstanding performance by an animal on television or in film, and was the equivalent of an actor winning an Oscar."

"Was the Patsy only awarded to horses?"

"Any animal actor was eligible."

"What other horses have won the Patsy?"

"The first Patsy was awarded to Francis, the talking mule, who also worked with Les Hilton. Francis made many comedy films. Trigger won the Patsy for his role in *Son of Pale Face,* as did Diamond in *Flame of Arabia,* and California in *The Palomino.* I don't know why, but the Patsy has not been awarded for many years, which is unfortunate because animal actors appreciate the recognition and would like to see the Patsy Award ceremony return."

"Have any actors won awards because of their horses?"

"Gene Autry and Champion, Roy Rogers and Trigger, and Tom Mix and Tony are the only human-horse partnerships to put their hand and hoof prints beside one another on the Hollywood Walk of Fame.

"Lee Marvin credited Smokey, the horse that could stand with his front legs crossed while supporting a hung-over Kid Shelleen, for his Oscar-winning role in *Cat Ballou*. Smokey also received an award of his own, the Craven, for his work in that movie."

"What is the Craven Award?"

"It was named for Robert Craven, an animal lover and the first director of the American Humane Association office in Hollywood. The Craven Award was bestowed annually to an animal actor that was well-trained and displayed unique talents during filming."

"You said 'was.' Does that mean the Craven is also no longer given?"

"Unfortunately yes, and we wish the Craven would be awarded again."

"What horses have won the Craven?"

"The Lone Ranger's Silver, Flicka, Bracket, Fury, Outlaw, and the amazing stunt horse, Jerry Brown, who worked with a great trainer of the same name."

"Do you have a favorite action sequence?"

"The chariot race in the second *Ben Hur*. That spectacular sequence was rehearsed for six months and took more than six weeks to film. Amazingly, only a few horses received minor bumps and bruises, because Yakima Canutt, a former silent screen actor turned stuntman then director, carefully choreographed the complicated scene. Mr. Canutt was an animal lover and one of the first stuntmen who really cared for horses' well-being and safety. Many horses, including extras, were brought from all over Europe and patiently trained to draw chariots, first in pairs, then three at a time, and finally, four abreast."

"Where did the four white stallions that Mr. Heston drove come from?"

"Altair, Rigel, Antares, and Aldebaran were magnificent Lipizzaners from Austria."

"Did Charleton Heston actually drive the chariot?"

"Yes, but Mr. Heston only drove the horses in a straight line. Mr. Canutt trained stunt drivers to do the rest of the racing."

"What about all the crashes and pile-ups?"

"They frequently used dummy horses and very short action shots to capture exciting footage without exposing the horses to danger."

"What other actors and equines formed close friendships?"

"Just like Billy Crystal bought me, Viggo Mortensen purchased T.J., who portrayed Hidalgo in the movie of the same name. And Tom Cruise bought Felix, his dependable charger in the movie, *The Last Samurai.*"

I massaged Beechnut's back and thanked him. He looked over his shoulder and asked, "Did you bring something for me?"

Remembering the bag of baby carrots in the car, I excused myself, paused to ask the manager for permission to give some to Beechnut, and returned with the treats, which he greatly relished.

"Is acting the most important work horses do?" I asked.

"We think one to one equine-assisted therapy is the most important job," mused Beechnut. "Please get to know some therapy horses. I suggest that you volunteer at a therapeutic riding center."

"Horses change lives. They give our young people confidence and self-esteem. They provide peace and tranquility to troubled souls— they give us hope!"

- TONI ROBINSON

THERAPY HORSES

Jan and Rev;
Steamboat Springs, Colorado

Humble Ranch Education and Therapy Center, a non-profit therapeutic riding organization located in Steamboat Springs, is a member of the North American Handicapped Riding Association (NAHRA). Founded in 1969, NAHRA has a membership of more than six hundred enterprises that support therapeutic equine programs for people with special needs. Across the Yampa River from the center, Mt. Werner rises to ten thousand feet. South of Humble Ranch, the broad grassy valley stretches toward distant mountains cloaked in aspen and pine.

I met with Cheri, the director of the center, in the one-hundred-year-old ranch house and related the horses' mission and their request to include a chapter about equine therapy. I offered to volunteer. Cheri graciously invited me to visit the horses anytime and gave me a handbook that provided guidelines describing the responsibilities of side walkers and lead walkers. The horses and Cheri would train me for both positions. She said that people from all walks of life volunteer to help. However, to assist effectively, volunteers must be in touch with their gentler side and be willing to learn from horses.

Six therapy horses casually grazed in a field, and four others, anxious to join their partners, shuffled about in a roomy paddock. I followed Cheri to the barn's tack room. Saddle racks, with pads and English and Western saddles, neatly lined one wall. Lead ropes, halters, and bridles hung on hooks made from old horseshoes. Above the hooks were the names and photographs of each horse; below were their grooming buckets. Clipboards held a list of the equipment used with each horse and a therapy schedule.

In the paddock, Cheri introduced to me to Buster, Little Buck, Rev, and Jan, the senior therapy horses at Humble Ranch. I introduced myself and let each one smell my hands and face before I handed out baby carrots.

I asked Cheri why the horses were separated when they seemed anxious to join the others. She smiled and responded that the four in the paddock had just been ridden and were cooling down.

Maximilian, Raven, Bubba, Doc, Buckshot, and Sir munched fresh grass in the field. At the sound of crunching carrots, several lifted their heads and swiveled their ears in interest.

Buster was a friendly, white Arabian pony with light reddish dappling over his entire body. Approaching thirty, Buster was the oldest member of the ranch's equine family, but he still loved giving therapy rides. When he took the treat, I noticed a deep impression on his forehead. He told me that he had been kicked by another horse before coming to the ranch.

Buster said that his previous owner had kept him and four other horses in a very small paddock. An odd number of horses meant that one horse did not have a pair bond mate. One evening, Buster was first in line for food, but two of the other horses chased him away. Since he had no one to protect his off side, he didn't see the hoof that nearly killed him. Buster whispered that he loved being at Humble Ranch, because the people were very nice and there was an even number of horses, which meant that everyone had an equine best friend.

Little Buck was the second to oldest member of the family. The pretty, little dun-colored pony had a black mane and tail, a thin brown dorsal stripe, and black zebra stripes on his legs. He said that he was a descendent of the ancient Przewalzki horses of Mongolia. Little Buck's right eye was missing and his ribs were clearly visible through his coat. I asked him why he was so thin. Little Buck replied that he had had a tumor. Both the growth and his eye had to be surgically removed. He said that he was recovering and trying to gain weight. Little Buck added that he was sometimes frightened when someone approached from his right side without vocalizing, but he still enjoyed giving therapy rides to children.

Jan, a lovely golden palomino, was the senior mare at Humble Ranch. Her equine best friend, the strawberry roan Reverence—Rev for short—was the tallest. Both were in their mid-twenties. Jan loved to work with children; Rev preferred adults.

The affection among the horses and people at Humble Ranch created a palpable atmosphere of love, nurturing, and cooperation. I visited the ranch often to let the horses know and trust me. Sometimes, I would just hang out and hand out treats or give massages, so the horses would get used to my touch. I even joined Jan in the paddock and took naps using her belly as a pillow. At other times, I would sit at their feet and read a chapter of this book to them.

At first, the horses allowed me to concentrate on learning my role as a walker, so they spoke little about the history of equine therapy. Training taught me to properly assist the horses, so that they could act freely as equine therapists for their human students.

Staying in the moment is the most important lesson for volunteers to learn: clearing one's mind of all other thoughts; concentrating on individual needs, abilities, and personalities; and keen observation. This enables the students to receive the maximum benefit from equine healing and ensures a successful experience for all involved in a therapy session.

The side walker's job is to maintain focus on the student's safety, select the appropriate helmet, introduce the student to the horse and the lead walker, and remain in close proximity throughout the therapy session to assist if an emergency dismount is necessary. The side walker also assists the medical practitioner to ensure that riders reach their goals. At the end of the ride, the side walker helps the student dismount and gives the horse a treat.

The lead walker's job is to fetch the therapy horse that has been matched with a student, assess the horse's health during grooming, and tack up the equine according to the student's needs. In the arena, they warm up by practicing the routine to be used and familiarizing themselves with objects such as wooden bridges, poles on the ground in various configurations, and barrels. The horse is then ready to greet the student.

During riding class, the lead walker focuses on the entire group's safety by observing the layout of the arena, the other therapy groups, and the spectators. The lead walker remains constantly mindful of anything that might distract or upset the horse.

A good lead walker keeps the horse relaxed and attentive to the student during therapy. Once, I led a trail ride during which the equine therapist, Bud, lightly nipped my forearm, because I was paying more attention to the beautiful scenery than to our rider. The gentle reminder left no bruise, but refocused my attention on our student. Bud's sensitivity to our student's needs was impressive.

After a class, the lead walker allows the horse to cool down. Because every equine therapy session is unique, it is a continual learning process for every horse and person involved. Sometimes students make great progress in a single session. Other times, improvement is almost imperceptible, but each individual's performance is recorded, and treatment is adjusted.

One of the most essential aspects of every therapy class is the joy each student experiences from being around horses. Many spirits are lifted even before clients are introduced to their equine partner. Some students regard the horses as nonjudgmental friends, rather than therapists.

After numerous friendly visits and several months of assisting with therapy rides, I spent an afternoon with Jan and Rev in a paddock. While grooming and massaging them, I asked, "Who was the first horse healer?"

"The first horse healers sadly were sacrifices. For thousands of generations, people barbarically sacrificed humans, horses, and other animals to provide comfort and to serve as guides for a deceased person's journey to the next world.

"Old Bob was one of the first modern-day horse healers to be remembered for the services he provided," answered Jan thoughtfully. "Old Bob and Abraham Lincoln were longtime friends. The dedicated steed carried young Mr. Lincoln around Illinois, which enabled him to expand his law practice. The long friendship culminated when Old Bob accompanied the assassinated President's funeral procession. Slowly the rider-less horse followed the carriage, symbolizing an ancient tradition of mourning a leader who would ride no more. Seeing Old Bob walk behind his departed friend comforted many people. One hundred years later, Black Jack, a celebrated military mount, provided similar psychological support to millions of people as he followed President Kennedy's casket."

"Comanche was another great healing horse," added Rev. "He was Captain Keogh's military mount and close companion. Comanche was the only survivor found by the United States Cavalry after the battle at Little Big Horn, where General Custer and his company of more than two hundred men died, just two weeks before America's one-hundredth birthday.

"During the battle, many soldiers killed their horses to use as shields, but not Captain Keogh. After the encounter, Indians took the few surviving horses, but they could not approach Comanche, who refused to leave his fallen friend. Days later, Comanche was found lying next to the body of Captain Keogh. Although Comanche was too weak to stand, the troops were determined to save his life. Usually a horse in such poor condition would be euthanized.

"In a hospital, alongside soldiers, Comanche was nursed back to health. He was retired with full military honors and never ridden again. He crisscrossed the country by train for many years to visit soldiers' families and friends, thereby providing them a connection to their absent loved ones."

"How did one on one equine-assisted therapy begin?"

"Some people think it began with Franklin Roosevelt," answered Jan. "President Roosevelt once told Prime Minister Churchill that horseback riding helped him deal with the long hours he spent in a wheelchair, due to polio. He said that riding improved his balance and strengthened his muscles. Mr. Churchill replied with the now famous statement, 'There's something about the outside of a horse that's good for the inside of a man.' "

Rev added, "Teddy Roosevelt, who was President twenty years before Franklin, was an asthmatic. He claimed that riding outdoors was great therapy for his asthma. With the help of horses, he conquered his condition.

"Actually horses have indirectly provided treatment for humans long before most people acknowledged equines' therapeutic potential. In ancient times, Hippocrates, the father of modern medicine, observed the flora eaten by horses. In this way, he could safely experiment with those plants and determine their medicinal benefits for people. The Greeks, Romans, Germans, and French have used horses to transport handicapped people for centuries. When Liz Hartel and Jubilee won silver medals in the Olympics in the 1950s, the entire world recognized the therapeutic value of horses.

"Like Franklin, Liz also had polio, yet she and her horse successfully competed in the largest sporting event in the world against able-bodied men and women. Liz and Jubilee were leaders, and in the saddle, no one realized that Liz had various physical impediments. With Jubilee's help, Liz reclaimed many of the motor skills she had lost, though she still remained paralyzed below her knees. Despite that, the two close companions traveled the world and gave dressage demonstrations. That pair was undeniable proof that horses help humans heal.

"Throughout history, those examples and many more evolved into the growing movements of hippotherapy, therapeutic riding, and more recently, horses being recognized as mental health providers. Remember, every relationship is unique, so a myriad of possibilities for healing exists."

"How do hippotherapy and therapeutic riding differ?"

"Hippotherapy is when a student receives treatment through a horse's movements in accordance with a therapist's program. Personalized exercises improve a rider's flexibility and strength. People may ride backwards, or lie sideways across the saddle, to stretch and strengthen their bodies. Some people need two side walkers, or an instructor may ride behind the student to provide physical support and encouragement. Whereas, therapeutic riding increases the students' physical fitness levels and develops their cognitive abilities while they learn to direct the horse.

"We assist with many different emotional, physical, and learning challenges, which affect children and adults, including autism, cerebral palsy, multiple sclerosis, muscular dystrophy, paralysis, spina bifida, Alzheimer's disease, amputees, terminal illness, and many more. People who are blind, deaf, or incarcerated often feel isolated from other people. Their contact with an animal establishes a therapeutic relationship that gives them a reason to live and interact in society. Horses believe that all people benefit from spending time with a horse, because in caring for an animal, a mutual bond develops that benefits both beings. And scientific research has proven that people who connect with animals live longer, healthier, and more fulfilling lives."

"How do horses help blind people?"

"The Guide Horse Foundation, based in North Carolina, trains miniature horses, who are the size of a large dog, to function like Seeing Eye dogs."

"Why train horses when we have dogs?"

"Seeing Eye dogs do a great job, but there are more than one million blind people in North America alone, and less than one percent has a guide animal. Since animal vision providers often become a sightless person's best friend, it is distressing to lose a dog after eight or ten years. Guide horses have up to three times the working life of a dog, so it makes psychological as well as economic sense to use guide horses. The training of guide dogs and horses is similar. Imagine having to train only one horse versus three dogs per person."

"Do guide horses have limitations as to where they can go?"

"Their hooves are fitted with soft shoes so as not to damage floors. When guide horses are indoors, they will signal their need to eliminate and wait to be taken outside. Plus, they can be outfitted with panniers to carry groceries and small packages."

"Do miniature horses help people in other ways?"

"The Rising Star Rehabilitation Center in Colorado offers free programs, specifically designed for challenged children and seniors, which focus on patient interaction with tiny horses for rehabilitative therapy."

"How many equine therapy centers exist?"

"There are over a thousand centers in more than forty countries; England and America have more than nine hundred of those programs. Every center is unique, though national associations, like NAHRA, in North America, and Riding for the Disabled, in England, have adopted universal standards for treatment. In fact, equine-assisted therapy has produced many miracles. Every center has wonderful stories about people making spectacular improvements. In some cases, the medical community had given up hope for the patients."

"Please tell me about the miracles."

"Children over six years old, who had never spoken in their lives, have uttered their first words while riding. It has been documented several times—including here at Humble Ranch. In several cases, doctors told the parents of children with special needs that their child would never walk. Some began walking after horseback riding. For example, the Diamond Center was established more than thirty years ago, because the power of a horse helped a child with spina bifida learn to walk. The center is currently the largest facility of its kind in the world and conducts more than four hundred therapy riding and driving sessions per week. That feat was recently repeated at the Chigwell Riding Trust, which is considered the world's first therapeutic riding center. One spring a few years ago, a seven-year-old boy took the first wobbly steps on his own after a therapy ride. His mother fainted, having been told by numerous doctors that her son would never walk.

"But my favorite miracle was performed by Negev," said Jan. "He worked at the Red Mountain Therapeutic Riding Center in southern Israel. Negev gave therapy rides to people from Egypt, Jordan, and Israel, regardless of their religious affiliation. Humans are all the same in our eyes—if a person is in need, we want to help.

"Negev provided therapy for one little boy who was blind and deaf. The child had never displayed any emotion in his entire life, but the first time on Negev's back, the child's laughter echoed around the arena. His positive display of emotion filled the spectators' eyes with tears and gave hope to all who heard him laugh."

"I am inspired most by Trianero," Rev commented. "He was a close companion to Adele and Marlena McCormick, who are mother and daughter psychotherapists. A brave pair, they help challenged people after all others have given up hope.

"One of their unique and innovative programs paired their favorite horse, Trianero, with a teenaged boy who had lost his will to live. The charger provided the boy comfort when others could not. Through love, patience, and understanding, Trianero formed a very close connection with the troubled teenager.

"Unfortunately, the youth's deep despair was so intense that he decided to end his life with a shard of glass. But the teenager felt compelled to say good-bye to his favorite friend first. Inside Trianero's paddock, the boy displayed his weapon to imply his intent. The stallion stepped forward and knocked the shard from the boy's hand. This caused such a welling-up of emotion that the boy dissolved into tears and sobbingly fell asleep under Trianero's protection. The next morning, the astounded McCormicks witnessed an amazing alteration in the youth's personality. A new, positive life force had emerged in the boy, who until that time no one felt had any chance for happiness.

"And those are just a few cases. To us, every time a horse brings a smile to the face of a challenged child or adult, we consider it a miracle, because that person's smile means we have touched a soul. And that one smile also uplifts the volunteers, the therapist, and the parents. Thus, horses provide therapy simultaneously for many people by inspiring hope and healing in ways that other human interventions are incapable of achieving."

Then Jan asked, "Would you like to hear what some people with special needs have told the horses about therapeutic riding?"

"That would be great."

"One person with multiple sclerosis told me that she is limited when she is on the ground, but not on a horse. On a horse, she feels overjoyed and in control, and she forgets about her disease. Another rider divulged that he feels a strong connection through the rhythm of each therapy horse he rides. He said horses speak directly to his heart, and that they sense his blindness. And a woman said that after she had ridden away from her wheelchair for the first time, even though she would have to return to it, she would never be the same. A whole new dimension had been added to her life, which, until that moment, had seemed impossible to her."

Rev added, "We heard about a man with muscular dystrophy in England, who had been in a wheelchair since the age of two. As an adult, he was invited to try therapy riding. He never thought he could ride, but with the help of friendly volunteers, an expert instructor, and a steadfast horse, he gained enough strength and balance in the saddle to ride out of the arena into the countryside alone. As the disease progressed, he drove a horse-drawn carriage while still seated in his wheelchair and felt the same unbounded exhilaration.

"I remember a letter from the mother of a special student, which was read aloud to a group of volunteers. It was about her son, Ben, who was born with an undiagnosed syndrome, which caused chronic health problems, mental retardation, and various physical disabilities, such as difficulty standing upright and walking properly.

"Ben is now nine years old and has been riding for six years. Initially, Ben's riding instructor had to sit behind him on the horse. As he advanced, he learned to sit and balance on his own. For the past few years, Ben has been able to ride alone. On horseback, the motion of the horse's gait stimulates the muscles and nerves that are necessary for walking. This has led to a great improvement in his posture and walking ability. Riding also gives Ben a sense of achievement, and the advantage of seeing the world from a higher position. The letter concluded by thanking the people and horses at the center for never giving up hope for Ben, even though doctors thought his situation was hopeless."

"Why are horses such special healers?"

"All animals have the potential to help humans heal in various ways. A major difference between horses, cats, and dogs is that, with an equine, the person learns by living in the horse's environment, whereas with a cat or dog, the human's home or care center is where the healing takes place. A horse may be ten or twenty times the weight of a person and still treat that individual, no matter what the challenges are, with nonjudgmental dignity, patience, and love, all of which instill within a person a sense of self-worth, self-respect, and ultimately, self-acceptance.

"Being astride a horse broadens a person's perspective by giving a new, uplifting point of view. And besides the fun a person may have, riding exercises every muscle in the human body. Having the ability to guide and work with an equine friend is empowering.

"The magic of equine therapy is that through love, patience, and fun, a person can be transformed. A challenged rider, who feels acceptance, begins to respond differently to other living creatures. Giving and accepting love has inspired students with a will to live and a desire to love themselves, as well as others."

"Why is fun so important for therapy?"

"Someone once said that laughter is the best medicine," stated Jan. "Having fun is expressed through laughter. For some people, the fun starts before the ride—they are happy just to see the horses. Others make a magical metamorphosis the moment they mount and ascend to new heights physically and emotionally. Plus, the therapist offers games for the students while they are riding. Those games improve a person's physical and cognitive abilities and make riding even more enjoyable, because many forget they are in therapy.

"As equine therapists, we experience pleasure when we feel and hear the person's elation while driving or riding. Nothing makes us feel better about ourselves than hearing a person's laughter during a healing session."

"Do therapy horses need special training?"

"Definitely. While almost every horse has healing capabilities, not every horse is ready to serve at an equine therapy center, because horses, like people, are unique individuals. We have to learn to be patient, with several years of experience dealing with people, before we can work at an equine therapy center. When we do enter the therapy field, we are trained to be impervious to distractions and improper commands."

"Are there other types of equine therapy?"

"Yes, there are many, including the rapidly-expanding field of equine-assisted mental health healing, which the McCormicks helped to pioneer. Plus, there are hundreds of equestrian events for people with unique challenges, which culminate with the Special Olympics and Paralympic Games. These worldwide sporting spectacles include equestrian events, which show the world how capable people can be, in spite of the huge hurdles they confront.

"Other programs also deserve recognition. For example, the Inner City Slickers, founded by Michael McMeel, who, inspired by the movie City Slickers, created a program that helps disadvantaged children. The Inner City Slickers hosts events at its ranch and visits detention centers and juvenile halls in cities throughout California. Through their programs, thousands of at-risk young people and gang members, many of whom had never previously touched or seen an equine up close, have received valuable lessons from horses.

"In grooming and feeding the horses, participants learn responsibility. Considering the needs of another being helps to develop respect for an individual, unconditional acceptance, and a bond of trust. When the youths learn to feel and express compassion and love through their interactions with horses, they make positive internal transformations that affect them forever.

"Several prisons have also developed equine therapy programs. While each curriculum might be slightly different, the lessons learned by the inmates are universal: self-confidence, self-discipline, and self-esteem. Acquiring these traits enables inmates to more successfully rejoin society. In some instances, participating inmates experience love from another being for the first time and make dramatic personality improvements as a result of their interactions with horses.

"We love helping all kinds of people, but in many cities there are few opportunities for people to play with horses. That concerns us greatly. For example, it is appalling that given the millions of people who live and work in Manhattan, the only public stable left, the Claremont Riding Academy, recently closed. Unfortunately, this left the New York Therapeutic Riding Center, which leased horses and space from the stable and had a waiting list as long as my leg, no place to operate.

"The Claremont Riding Academy was the oldest continuously-operated stable in the United States. Sadly, New York City is rife with millions of overly stressed people, and there are only a few carriage, police, and pleasure horses left to help them. Most large cities severely lack interactive equine opportunities to assist in human spiritual growth. In fact, many cities have more statues of horses than they have live horses, which only makes it more important to preserve stables like the Vauxhall City Farm."

"Where is the Vauxhall City Farm?"

"It is located in the heart of London—a short walk from the Thames River. People in Vauxhall established the community-supported two-acre farm so that children might interact with farm animals such as chickens, goats, pigs, cows, and horses. Four of the horses there are specially trained to give free therapy rides.

"John Anthony Davies, a great equine therapy enthusiast, poignantly captures the ultimate dream of therapy horses:

> I saw a child who couldn't walk,
> sit on a horse, laugh and talk.
> Then ride it through a field of daisies
> and yet he could not walk unaided.
> I saw a child, no legs below,
> sit on a horse, and make it go
> through woods of green
> and places he had never been
> to sit and stare,
> except from a chair.

I saw a child who could only crawl
mount a horse and sit up tall.
Put it through degrees of paces
and laugh at the wonder in our faces.
I saw a child born into strife,
take up and hold the reins of life
and that same child was heard to say,
Thank God for showing me the way...

I thanked Jan and Rev for their inspirational stories and asked them about the horses' hopes for humanity.

Jan replied, "Please go see Sundance and ask him about the horses' hopes for helping humans save the Earth."

"Horses represent the other part of self,
the child-like innocence and openness to all things new,
what we want to be. When we are open to them,
they bring us back to our deeper selves."

- HILDEGARD GEORGE

THE HORSES' HOPES

Sundance; Steamboat Lake,
Colorado

Snow fell lightly as I drove to Bess's pasture. All my tension melted away as I rounded the partially frozen lake. A mist rose from its edges, similar to the morning when I first met Bess. This was her pasture—difficult to believe so many months had passed since she had left it.

Near the edge of the water, a gust of wind blew up a swirl of snow. As the flakes unfurled, a shiver tingled down my spine. Then the wind ceased, and the swirling snow settled, leaving me feeling melancholy, yet caressed by Bess' indomitable spirit. I thanked Bess for asking me to write the horses' story.

Suddenly beside me, Sundance asked, "You miss my mom?"

"Yes," I responded softly as a tear ran down my cheek. We stood silently side by side. Sometimes, between close friends, no words are necessary.

I wiped the tear away and was grateful to have Sundance as a guide. The snow had stopped; sunrays shone brilliantly on distant white-capped peaks. After a long silence, I hugged Sundance and asked, "How is your family?"

Pleased, he introduced me to his son, Sammy, a smaller image of his father. Plus, there was a new filly in the band, Becky. Both were very cute playing together as the adults kept a watchful eye. And although Bess and another adult horse had passed away, the births of Becky and Sammy kept the band in balance.

"Sundance, it's great to see you and the new foals," I said while passing out carrots and hugging my friends. The energized horses happily gathered for the treats.

I asked Sundance about the horses' hopes.

"Humans and horses are supposed to be together. You have learned that equines have helped people in almost every human endeavor. In your travels around the world, was it easier to communicate with equines or humans?"

"Equines," I answered, and several horses nickered.

"While humans have several thousand languages, horses have only one. What has that taught you?" asked Sundance.

"That anyone can commune with horses."

"Yes, people just have to be receptive and understand our needs."

"What does a horse need?"

"Horses and humans share the same emotions and require the same basic things: love, companionship, food, and freedom. We need love from other horses and from people. We want to be with other horses, because isolation undermines our physical and psychological well-being. Equines need healthy food and opportunities to run and play at liberty.

"Sundance, what are your thoughts on riding?"

"If you want to be a good rider, you first need to earn our respect and trust. Most people mount a horse too soon. Focus on building a relationship. Spend time with your horse as you would a best friend. Don't be in a hurry; have fun and be patient.

Make an equine's needs your needs. Tell a horse what you are going to do before doing it. Gaining a horse's trust, before riding, is easier on the rider and the ridden. True equestrians know that a horse's well-being should be the rider's primary concern.

"Also, equines prefer being ridden without a bit or other hobbles, but if used, realize that the same reins in different hands can be heaven or hell. Please have soft hands, because our mouths are very sensitive. Remember that it is much easier to lose than to gain an equine's respect. We love to play with a person we trust, which helps to develop a tighter bond.

"There are two ways to teach a horse. One is through communication and compassion; the other is through fear and intimidation. Horses use reason to make choices based on learned experiences. It is the person who has to learn how to be a rider. A horse without a rider is still a horse; a rider without a horse is no longer a rider. It's not about being right or in control; it's about being kind, caring, and creating a loving partnership. Remember, in riding a horse, a person is borrowing freedom from a horse. When a rider falls off and calls a horse stupid, that person should really look in the mirror. Keep in mind that riding is a risky sport. If you ride, you may fall."

"What are some other equine aspirations?"

"We want people to respect all life! Many people still believe that animal consciousness is inferior or doesn't exist at all, which makes humans less responsible for the cruelties they impose on us. Millions of domestic cattle, pigs, and chickens are kept on factory farms in inhumane conditions. Many never see the light of day or stand on natural earth until just before they are slaughtered for human consumption. We also detest the way animals are treated during experiments. Most drug- and product-testing on animals is cruel and unnecessary. People need to recognize animals as fellow sentient beings and ensure that they live in humane surroundings.

"We want humans to stop the slaughter of hundreds of thousands of healthy horses each year. We are thankful for places like the Home of Rest for Horses, in England, the Kettlemont Home for Thoroughbreds, in America, and Pech Petite, in

France. We hope many more places like these are established, because we want every horse to live a long life filled with love, joy, and tender care.

"Horses hope that people continue to research ways to help us recover from illness or injury, by incorporating holistic care with traditional medicine. Humans have caused the extinction of flora and fauna throughout the world. Equines hope that people will preserve the remaining habitats. We must save every part of the natural world, because therein lies the answer to all the ills that affect the Earth and its living beings.

"Our highest aspiration is to partner with women and to empower them, because women will help to save the world by redirecting humanity onto a more peaceful, life-sustaining path. We want all women's dreams to come true. Throughout the ages, domineering men have thwarted women's opportunities to reach their full potential. If men continue to rule the world alone, we are all in trouble. The world needs more strong, empathetic women, in positions of authority, to re-establish the balance between beings and the environment."

"How can people partner with a horse?"

"What were you doing when you first heard Bess?"

"I was enjoying an amazing sunrise."

"You were also living in the moment. This is a trait that all animals possess. Humans have mostly forgotten how to live in the moment, because they're too busy dreaming about the future or contemplating the past."

"What does it feel like to live in the moment?"

"Life just seems to flow. Time becomes immaterial, because you are totally engrossed in your surroundings, and in what you are doing at that moment. But, by consciously trying to identify when you are in the moment, you may lose the essence of actually existing solely in the present."

"How do people learn to live in the moment?"

"The path is different for each. People have to find out what works for them. One has to be focused without consciously focusing. Trying to force a connection, and a fear of failure, are the surest ways to miss the moment.

"Major keys to success involve amplifying feelings of love and exercising patience. Be calm, relax, and go slowly. Keep writing materials nearby to record your thoughts, feelings, impressions, and questions. Be cognizant of your body and learn to know yourself. What are your emotional and physical strengths and weaknesses? How would you like to improve your life? Record your responses and relay them to your equine partner, for there are many ways that a horse can help a human, if a person is willing to ask.

"On a regular basis, seek out solitude by spending time in nature and expressing your appreciation for all of its wonders. Show gratitude; practice kindness and forgiveness for yourself as well as others. Try different kinds of meditation, chanting, or prayer and select the ones that you enjoy. Engage in recreation for good health, have fun, and laugh.

"Realize that all matter is electrical energy, and that we are all related. One can stimulate a more aligned state by incorporating pictures or figurines of horses to adorn one's home. Place a bird feeder or two outside your dwelling. Birds are a great link to nature and an equine's friends, because we love their songs, rely on them as sentries, and they help keep annoying insects away. Birds do the same around a human's home."

"Where does a person start?"

"An important ingredient, for partnering with an equine, is to try to see the world from our viewpoint. Imagine seeing what we see, hearing what we hear, feeling what we feel, and sensing what we sense. "

"Please describe a horse's vision."

"Eyes are the only uncovered part of the brain and are windows to the soul. Our large eyes give us good night vision. Since our eyes are located on the sides of our heads, we can see almost everything around us without moving, which is very important for a prey animal. Although we have two small blind spots: one directly behind us, and the other at the end of our noses. Thus, equines cannot actually see what we put in our mouths, so a person has to be careful when feeding horses by hand.

"When relaxed, we see what is on our left side through the left eye as one picture, and an instant later, we see what is on our right side through our right eye as a separate picture. What we see from each eye is two dimensional, like a photograph, which makes it very difficult to tell how far away an object or predator may be. That is why quick movements or distant objects can startle an equine, and why things that are not really a threat can easily spook horses. The only time a horse has binocular vision and depth perception is when looking directly at a subject with both eyes.

"An equine's eyes, just like a human's, reveal the horse's disposition. Seeing the whites of the eyes, or a steely stare, indicates that the horse is upset or fearful. Whereas, a soft eye is a welcoming sign.

"How keen is a horse's hearing?"

"Compared to people, our hearing is hypersensitive. An equine's ears can swivel around independently, which increases our auditory skill. The physical position of our ears silently transmits our alertness to others. When we are relaxed, our ears are upright and slowly swivel about. When our ears are pointed in the same direction, we are alert to a particular sound. If our ears are laid back flat, it means that we are angry or upset.

"Equines use their entire body to communicate. Pay close attention to our body positioning. If we face you, that is generally a friendly gesture; when we present our hindquarters first, we might be upset. Even the way we move our tails have different meanings. Swishing is a happy display, whereas shaking means we are annoyed, or it can be that we are just chasing a fly away.

"You can study the nuances of body language by spending quiet time with your equine friend and teacher. Through patience and careful observation of subtle changes, you will learn a horse's non-verbal communications."

"What about a horse's sense of smell?"

"Every breath brings in new aromas and messages, because equines breathe exclusively through our noses. In fact, we can tell a lot about a person by sharing breath with someone. Once a human and a horse are properly acquainted, a person may softly exhale near a horse's nostril. One whiff can reveal a lot to a horse about a person's state of well-being."

"How sensitive is a horse to touch?"

"We can sense a fly landing on our body, and we can twitch the underlying muscle to chase it away. Horses greatly enjoy gentle grooming and stroking by other horses and by humans. We prefer stroking and scratching to patting or slapping, because soft strokes replicate grooming between horses, an act of mutual caring. Many horses return a person's soft strokes by scratching people with their lips and teeth, which is a gesture of love."

"What sounds do horses use to communicate?"

"Domestic horses are more vocal than our wild African cousins. A horse may nicker to say hello or to invite you to approach. We also use a neigh or a whinny to say, 'Hi, it's me,' or to tell you where we are. A blowing sound is asking for attention, whereas snorting expresses interest or just confirms our well-being. When a horse roars, it is conveying fear or anger, and a screaming stallion is expressing his bravado to another.

"Remember, understanding the mechanics of the horse is science; listening to our soul is an art. I am explaining our body language, and the way in which our senses function, so that people learn to approach us with greater initial understanding and sensitivity. Then the communication process can begin."

"How does a person approach a horse?"

"If you want to partner with a horse, you must have the owner's or caregiver's permission. While looking for an equine best friend with whom to bond, realize that it may not be the first or second horse you meet. Express your intention and let the horse choose you. Horses like to have a purpose and to make lasting relationships. Helping their human friend provides that fulfillment.

"It is very important to have an open mind by erasing any preconceived ideas or expectations. Always remember that animals have emotions. If we didn't have individual feelings and personalities, we would all act the same.

"Horses are generally friendly animals, but mistreatment and fear may render some unpredictable. Caution should be used if you are unsure of a horse's temperament. Like people, we are unique individuals, although we share the desire for humane companions.

"Initially, just spend time with a horse. The most important lessons are learned when both horse and human have their feet on the ground. With little or no equine experience, a human can volunteer at a therapeutic riding center, a retirement home for horses, or a rescue center. Within these organizations, volunteers can seek out other compassionate people, who can teach them how to safely approach and interact with an equine.

"At the outset, people should introduce themselves in a calm, friendly voice and state their loving intentions to do no harm. The first time you meet a horse you might not even enter his paddock. Just enjoy and observe your new acquaintance, while continuing to express your love and appreciation. Let the horse make the next move.

"If the horse approaches you, let him smell the back of your hand. And if the horse stays calm, let him feel your light, loving touch. Continuing to speak softly, ask if he wants to interact with you. Then be open to his thoughts, sense his feelings, and notice his body language.

"When you enter a horse's paddock, you can visually demonstrate your non-threatening intentions by approaching the horse slowly from one side. A person may turn to show part of his or her back to the horse, a posture that signals a peaceful, non-aggressive intention.

"Remain calm, relax, and enjoy the moment of meeting a new, loving soul. Breathe deeply through your nose, smell the air, and feel it on your skin. Leisurely scan the horizon, absorbing everything, so that you know you and the horse are safe. Convey your loving feelings to the horse and assure his safety; he will start looking out for your safety, too. As you become more in tuned, practice synchronized breathing with your new friend. When you feel at ease, reaffirm to your equine friend that you respect him and are seeking his guidance and assistance."

"When will a person usually hear the horse?"

"After the human has become supersensitive to the surrounding environment, and when the person least expects it. The expression of the horse's love may be immediate, or it may take time to hear and sense the equine's words and emotions. Within a few days or weeks, it will happen.

"Once a friendship is established, your auras may overlap at any time. Keep in mind that horses want to find people who are seeking an equine companion, teacher, and guide. Remember, it is important to write down your animal companion's communications so that you will recall the equine's lessons later. Also, write down any questions, thoughts, and feelings you have for your equine partner so that you can share them.

"A person may ask an equine companion anything. Establish a dialogue with simple questions, such as; Are you healthy? Do you like it here? Is there anything you need or want? Who are your friends? What is your favorite activity, food, or place? Then progress to more substantive questions, which signify the sharing of feelings, such as; What do you think about humans? What do you think about me? What can we learn from each other? Note the horse's answer, which is usually the first thought that pops into your mind, an emotion you feel, or a mental image.

"If your mind wanders, acknowledge that thought, then refocus on the present interaction. Occasionally, bring treats. Baby carrots and quartered apples are the favorites."

"How can horses empower people?"

"Horses are joyous, warm, and energizing. We are also loyal, cheerful, gregarious, and extremely enthusiastic about living life. We value friendships, nurturing loved ones, and cultivating community bonds. Although all animals have healing potential for humans, the horse is special. In spite of our large size and great strength, we are a prey animal and identify greatly with women, whom we see as prey, compared to some men, who are more like predators. Equines can enhance a woman's innate intuition, patience, trust, and love. To horses, every human is precious, but we especially want to help women feel more confident by bonding with them. Horses accept every human as a unique individual—we do not judge the exterior, we judge what is inside. A person can be totally honest with a horse, because we will never reveal their secrets.

"People have lost much of their ability to relate to, and learn from, nature. Most domestic horses still know how to live in the wild. Horses encourage humans to coexist with the natural world.

"Just being with a horse reduces a person's blood pressure and stress level, and puts people more in touch with themselves and the moment, all of which helps them heal and grow. Loving a horse teaches humans love, respect, and appreciation for all life."

"What are the horses' goals in regard to women?"

"Horses love confident women. Our mission is to help women fully develop as individuals so that they can become compassionate leaders and teachers. Women leaders would shift a nation's values and priorities towards caring for the homeless, feeding and healing the people, cultivating peace rather than war, and preserving the environment.

"True change begins most often in one to one relationships; between a horse and a woman, a man and a woman, or between two women. Such partnerships ideally develop a woman's confidence, self-esteem, and self-respect. Horses also enhance women's physical fitness. When a woman's physical, mental, and emotional needs are balanced, her demand for integrity and intimacy in her individual relationships extends to all of her interactions with people, animals, and the Earth. Then, she is a fully empowered individual, who can institute change for herself, her family, her community, and her world.

"Even if a woman is in a relationship with a man, she still needs female companions, with whom to share common experiences. It's truly about women teaching women. Men teach women the man's way. Only women can support other women's practices of the feminine way. All women need other women in their lives to help empower them.

"Thus, we urge women to organize their own bands of female friends, which keep them balanced and instill the courage and support necessary to attain the goals that they cannot achieve alone. The power of the band also provides women with a safety net and allows them to share spontaneous joy and play, which are essential for one's well-being and spiritual growth.

"All beings' primary concern is for self-preservation. Horses help humans conquer many false fears, which is when erroneous bits of information appear real. We can help develop intuitive skills by teaching identification of innermost feelings, and appropriate responses to genuine life-threatening situations, such as abuse and assault.

"In the wild, equines do not tolerate abuse. Mares will not bond with an abusive stallion, and a disrespectful young male is expelled from the family unit. This isolated horse, now alone and exposed, quickly realizes his faults and amends his ways in order to be reintegrated with the band.

"Some of the most educated people seem mired in harmful attitudes and mistreatment of animals, women, children, and the Earth. The growing number of male horse whisperers, using a soft approach, gives horses hope that we can support all people in their relationships.

"Horses wish every person could have a supportive family. Although one can't choose one's family, a person can choose one's friends and equine partners. We want women to know, that in the wild, it is the female equine that chooses her mate. The male may pose the question, but it is the mare's decision to bond. We encourage women to take their time in selecting a companion, allowing a potential partner to repeatedly show evidence of his honest intentions. Best friends are partners. This is the equine way.

"Remember, horses thrive on helping humans. We are natural partners who have taken different courses. We need to reunite so that our combined path will lead to peace and love. Everyone has challenges that could be improved upon with the help of a horse. The support we provide is different for each. Sometimes, horses have more humanity than many humans, so we help people become more humane. Bonding with a horse brings the conscious and subconscious into closer alignment, allowing the cultivation and appreciation of a human's positive potential."

"What if a person has doubts about connecting with a horse?"

"Then that person should ask the equine companion more questions to help clarify or understand those feelings. Speaking with a horse's caregiver for confirmation about a horse's health, thoughts, or feelings may provide more feedback and greater understanding.

"All we ask is that humans give horses a chance to help them heal. At times, everyone is a solo traveler in the world, and having an honest equine friend is a real advantage. It's not about riding or being ridden. It's about love, friendship, and learning to let the positive, unique facets of your being shine.

"Equines want to help humans so much. We think Willis Lamm expresses our desire well:

> When you are tense, let me teach you to relax.
>
> When you are short tempered, let me teach you to be patient.
>
> When you are shortsighted, let me teach you to see.
>
> When you are quick to react, let me teach you to be thoughtful.
>
> When you are angry, let me teach you to be serene.
>
> When you feel superior, let me teach you to be respectful.
>
> When you feel self absorbed, let me teach you to think of greater things.
>
> When you are arrogant, let me teach you humility.
>
> When you are lonely, let me be your companion.
>
> When you are tired, let me carry the load.
>
> When you need to learn, let me teach you.
>
> After all, I am your horse.

"It is amazing to us that humans reach into outer space looking for new life, yet do not realize there is so much to learn about life here on Earth. How can humans communicate with beings from another planet, if they cannot understand their fellow creatures on this world?

"Our hope is that we can teach people to be more open-minded, to believe in themselves, and to treat all beings with respect. After all, humans call the planet "Mother Earth." Who better to preserve and protect our mother than humans living nurturing lives?"

Bud and Hal at Humble Ranch; Steamboat Springs, Colorado

"Horses leave hoof prints on your heart."

- H. A. LEVIN

Author's Notes

All of the places, the people, and all of the horses, who told the stories in this book, are real! I bought a ton of carrots for the horses and traveled around the world to visit with them. During that time, I never rode a horse. I groomed them, tacked them up, and led therapy-riding sessions. Frequently, my only desire was to spend time with my equine friends, walking in the fields, enjoying the day, and grooming the horses, while they remained at liberty. These practices allowed the horses to leave if they chose; rarely did they walk away.

People frequently ask how I learned to communicate with animals. In truth, I now realize that horses had been approaching me for more than twenty years, before I was open enough in my heart to hear their voices. In fact, for a long time, I feared horses because they were so big. My equine experiences have banished my fear, and filled me with love, admiration, and respect, while expanding those feelings to encompass all animals.

Anyone can learn to communicate with animals and feel their emotions. Some people can readily slip into an animal's consciousness and grasp its thoughts. Others will need to expunge preconceived ideas in order to achieve their goal. Accomplishing animal communication is easier than people think. Most animals are willing to connect with compassionate people and explore the many healing possibilities that interspecies communication affords.

However, in the animal kingdom, equines hold a unique position in their relationship with people. As you have read, horses have carried and pulled humans and their cargo many more miles than any other animal. Many have toiled their entire lives in excruciating conditions until their cruel demise. Yet horses remain solidly devoted to helping humanity.

Trying to be the voice for a hundred million horses was daunting at times. Whenever I was filled with doubt and insecurity about writing the horses' story, someone would come into my life to affirm my direction and give me the necessary emotional support to continue.

In order to help myself hear the horses' voices more readily, I attended animal communication seminars, read many books, meditated, and spent a lot of time in nature with equines. Linda Tellington-Jones and Margrit Coates are two authors, who helped me most in my approach to horses.

Generally, I found the human horse-lover community to be incredibly kind, caring, and giving. According to Equestrian Resources (EQR), over 75% of the members of all equine-related non-racing organizations in the United States are women, and more than 80% of the American Horse Show Association's (AHSA) members are female. Details of an American Horse Council study in 2002 reveal that more than seven million people are involved in the equine industry as horse owners, service providers, employees, and volunteers. More than four million people ride for recreation, and more than three million participate at horse shows.

However, some people, who consider themselves equine professionals insisted that I was spoiling the horses by giving them treats, and that I could not glean any information from equines. Some continue to maintain that a horse cannot think or feel, because its brain is only the size of a walnut. Those people cannot, or will not, open themselves to the equine reality. Horses are almost always willing to befriend humans, share their tales, and increase their workload in return for kind treatment—for if any animal deserves a little spoiling, it's horses. They are intrinsically linked to the history and advancement of the human race.

Horses are truly sentient beings, and their five senses are all more developed than ours, which makes it easier for them to live in the moment. Because I never knew when I would be receptive to hear, feel, or experience the horses' thoughts and feelings, I always carried a pocket-sized notebook. Several times, while driving, hiking, or biking, I would stop to record messages from equine friends. Although it is usually easier to communicate by first establishing a face to face relationship, there is no proximity parameter requirement with a telepathic connection. I have literally hundreds of photographs of horses with whom I have conversed, and a myriad of equine mementos, such as, horseshoes, carvings, and other symbols that spark my memory and put me in a relaxed, receptive state.

My meetings with horses yielded copious mini-messages. I say "mini" because most of my conversations with equines were brief in linear time. Horses are usually quite ready to converse with people if properly approached. It was I, who had trouble staying in the moment. Often, my conscious amazement at making contact with another species took me out of the moment. Yet sometimes, even the briefest connection resulted in a wealth of information, analogous to a picture being worth a thousand words. Several conversations ended an instant after they started; many times I failed to connect at all. Only when I had an open mind, free of the usual daily thoughts of life, would the horses' messages come. At times, I was astounded with the fluidity of conversation, and hours would pass like minutes. When I couldn't concentrate or focus, minutes seemed to stretch into hours.

It is easy to tell when a horse cares for you. Be patient and appreciate each horse as an individual. Horses and humans who bond often have similar background experiences, which enable them to heal each other. When you find the right horse, you will feel calm and relaxed in his presence. Accept and trust the horse and believe that a friendship will develop, even if your ability to trust has been abused. Through gentleness, genuine caring, patience, and an open mind—and offering a few treats—an understanding can be established. This will lead to trust, centering, and ultimately, enlightenment. Animal communication is within your grasp, if you believe it to be.

While horses rarely intentionally hurt humans, they are big animals and deserve respect and understanding. Horses, just like humans, can stumble or fall accidentally, so watch where you put your feet and where they put theirs.

A conscious expression of gratitude helps set the stage for living life in the moment. Animals experience gratitude, too; wealth, to equines, is the possession of family, friends, and health. Whenever I am with horses, in nature, or just feeling blessed, I utter a prayer that helps me center myself, "Thank you for all you have given us. Thank you for family, friends, health, and wealth. Thank you."

When you love and accept yourself, you are able to extend those feelings to others and enhance your consciousness. Ways to accomplish this include deciding to live the healthiest way possible: eat lots of fresh fruits, nuts, and vegetables; drink plenty of water; limit, or eliminate, the intake of meat. (Horses are vegetarians and appreciate when a human does not eat meat just before a visit. Equines do not like the smell of meat on a person's breath; they associate it with predators.) Exercise your body and mind every day. Relax, have fun, and remember that living a healthy lifestyle is a personal lifelong commitment.

Telling a horse your intentions, before acting on them, prepares the horse to be receptive. At the start of my research, some horses became startled when I took photographs of them. When I explained beforehand that I would like to take their picture, the horses usually settled, and some even posed by licking their lips, a gesture of friendship.

The message, "Love and peace is all we ask," appears repeatedly in my notes. Sometimes, the message is quoted directly from a horse. In other instances, these are the exact words that human companions have heard most often from their equine partners. A Mashatu Game Reserve Manager, Gregg, related that a zebra once followed the Reserve's vehicle for several miles, all the way into camp, then laid down to die peacefully. He swears he heard the zebra say, "Love and peace is all I ask."

A horse named Buckshot, who was donated to Humble Ranch to become a therapy horse, personally helped me the most. Buckshot and I connected immediately, and we had great fun together. He was young, tall, and fit. He had been named Buckshot because his light gray coat was generously dappled with dark spots. During the process of training him for therapeutic riding, I was diagnosed with a malignant melanoma on my knee. I was scheduled for surgery a few days later and had to temporarily forgo leading therapy rides at the ranch.

At home, the day after surgery, I was self-absorbed with having had cancer. The director at Humble Ranch called and said that Buckshot had been injured on the day of my operation. He had severely wounded himself on the sharp end of a metal post in the middle of a field. Surprisingly, his injury was in the same location as my incision, and we both required more than twenty stitches.

Buckshot's injury jolted me from my brooding depression and prompted a visit to my friend. Several stitches had already loosened in his nasty gash. My entire fist could have easily fit inside the gaping wound. I feared that Buckshot would never walk normally again. I returned to the ranch every day to tend to his injury. His recovery was remarkable—within a month he was dashing across the field as if nothing had happened. At the same time, he led me from despair and self-absorption back into the caring world. "Thank you, Buckshot."

Horses have maintained their steadfast devotion to people, because they know they can help restore humanity to its spiritual center and teach people to live more in the moment. Spending time with a horse will help you connect with Mother Nature and live a balanced and forgiving life: for yourself, for the other human lives that you touch, and for all living beings. Equines teach that to give is to receive.

People have created many artificial environments; our shelters and most of our foods are no longer natural. Our separation from nature has inhibited our spirituality and our ability to commune with the natural world and all of its creatures. A goal of living in the moment will revitalize the awareness of our interconnectedness to nature and all beings.

Horses have high hopes for connecting with people. Initially, I had no idea that horses could be my friends, guides, and teachers. They taught me to be myself, to help, not harm, to value my fellow beings, to love all creatures, and to play every day.

Anyone can hear and be helped by horses. The path is open, if you are willing to try.

"Throughout my life, there have been several occasions in which I found myself in awe of that which exists between women and horses."

- GaWaNi Pony Boy

Women Inspired By Horses

"Our perfect companions never have fewer than four feet."   - Colette

Throughout history, horses have helped many people, including artists, authors, actresses, activists, advocates, animal communicators, conservationists, cowgirls, doctors, educators, equestrians, entertainers, executives, healers, jockeys, Olympians, photographers, politicians, singers, songwriters, trainers, and veterinarians. These include, but are not limited to:

Clare Albinson	Kim Bassinger
Trina Bellack	Joan Benjamin
Mary L. Biennan	Gabrielle Boiselle
Josette Boon	Pam Brown
Dawn Brunke	Joanna Cannan
Mary Chapin Carpenter	Frankie Chesler
Patsy Cline	Margrit Coates

"I've seen so many people gravitate toward horses who had something going on emotionally that horses helped them with."   - MINI DAS

Nikki Cohen-Wichner	Ada Cole
Elaine Cordillo	Jasmine Crogan
Sheryl Crow	Mini Das
Julie Decker	Ellen DeGeneres
Bo Derek	Arti Doctor
Patricia M. Doennig	Hilary Duff
Monica Edwards	Dale Evans
Claudia Feh	Jane Fonda
Lanie Frick	Deborah Frowen
Temple Grandin	Michelle Grant
Susan F. Greaves	Kathleen Griffin
Lesley Harrison	Lorraine Harrison
Liz Hartel	Marguerite Henry

Her Royal Highness, Princess Anne of England

Her Majesty, Queen Elizabeth II of England

Her Majesty, Queen Victoria I of England

"The collective memories of horses and humans still intersect in intimate and highly emotional ways, even if contemporary human thought patterns and lifestyles strive to separate people from the rhythms of the natural world and its creatures"   - LINDA KOHANOV

"A pony is a childhood dream. A horse is an adult pleasure."

— Rebecca Carrol

Meridith Hodges	Judy Howard
Rachel Hunter	Maudie Hunter-Warfeild
Jean Ingelow	Linda Jennings
Velma Johnston	Martha Josey
Chaia King	Lisa Kiser
Linda Kohanov	Julie Krone
Jan-Marie Laude	Elizabeth Lindsay
Nicci Mackay	Judith Malotte
Kelly Marks	Neda de Mayo
Elizabeth Kaye McCall	Shirley MacLaine
Adele McCormick	Marlena McCormick
Vera McGinnis	Debbie McGillivray
Vickie Meisenburg	Mary Midkiff
Cathy Neelan	Annie Oakley
Sandra Day O'Connor	Jacqueline Kennedy Onassis
Caroline Plaisted	Melissa Pierson
Josephine Pullein-Thompson	Sandy Ransford
Sarah Lynn Richards	Susan Richards
LeAnn Rimes	Julia Roberts
Eleanor Roosevelt	Portia de Rossi
Jane Savoie	Barbra Schulte
Marion duPont Scott	Anna Sewell
Metha Shrum	Heather Simpson

"People ask me how I recovered from my eating disorder, and I have to say that horses really helped me. It shifted my focus and got me out to nature."

— Portia de Rossi

"Companionship with animals is the most precious aloneness there is."

- MARY BOSANQUET

Molly Siveright	Patricia Skinner
Debby Sly	Joelle Smith
Penelope Smith	Jan Snodgrass
Kate Solisti-Mattelon	Joyce Stranger
Julie Suhr	Sally Swift
Elizabeth Taylor	Jean M. Tebay
Linda Tellington-Jones	Shirley Temple
Bonnie Treece	Felicity Trotman
Cheri Trousil	Pip Unwin
Terry Ventura	Mary Wanless
Stacy Westfall	Patricia Wrightson

_____

And you

ACKNOWLEDGEMENTS

The equines' story could not have been written without the help of many people and many horses. Editors Dee Bolton and Gail Schisler were invaluable in helping me translate the horses' messages. Artist Daniella Thireou gave life to the horses' words with her illustrations.

Thank you to all of the people and equine professionals who freely gave their time and allowed me access to their beautiful steeds: Scott Campbell, Eleni Chioni, John A. Davies, Alan Day, Laura Dumbrell, Rick Frishman, Criss and John Fetcher, Mike Gochey, David Hancock, Nikki Katsouni, Amelia Kinkade, Sue Krauer, Willis Lamm, Phyllis and Mel Levin, Mary Littenauer, Eddie Maple, Pip Oliver, Sandra Olsen, Wendy Price, David Richardson, Hans Riegler, Linda Tellington-Jones, Margo Toulouse, Cheri and Ed Trousil, Pip Unwin, Sue Widick, and the staff at the Mashatu Game Reserve. And a heartfelt thank you to the patient horses for their inspiration and valuable lessons: the Ainos ponies, Astero, Barbie, Beechnut, Bess, Buckshot, Carlos, Cash, Enzo, Ecu, Europa, Flambeau, Gouveneur, Igloo, Indy, Jan, Jongleur, Kalin, Legend, Lolly, Lovely, Lupin, Luna, Reverence, Royal Samantha, Siamo, Sophie, Stanhope, Sundance, Suny, Touchdown, and the zebras in Botswana.

Grateful acknowledgement is made to the following for permission to reprint previously published and unpublished material.

John Anthony Davies: Poem "I Saw A Child" by John Anthony Davies. Reprinted by permission of the author.

Willis Lamm: Poem "Let me teach you" by Willis Lamm. Reprinted by permission of the author.

SUGGESTED READING

Albinson, Clare. *In Harmony with Your Horse.* Surrey, UK: Elliot Right Way Books, 1988.

Ball, Stefan, Heather Simpson, and Judy Howard. *Emotional Healing for Horses & Ponies.* Essex, UK: The C. W. Daniel Company Limited, 2001.

Blake, Henry. *Talking with Horses.* North Pomfret, Vt.: Trafalgar Square Publishing, 1975.

Boone, J. Allen. *Kinship with All Life.* New York: Harper & Row, 1954.

Brown, Dee. *The Gentle Tamers.* Lincoln, NE: University of Nebraska Press, 1958.

Brunke, Dawn. *Animal Voices.* Rochester, VT: Bear & Company/Inner Traditions International, 2002.

Budiansky, Stephen. *The Nature of Horses.* London: Phoenix/Orion Books Ltd, 1997.

Canfield, Jack, and Mark Victor Hansen. *Chicken Soup for the Horse Lover's Soul.* Deerfield Beach, FL: Health Communications, Inc., 2003.

Clutton-Brock, Juliet. *Horse Power.* Cambridge, MA: Harvard University Press 1992.

Coates, Margrit. *Healing for Horses.* London: Rider/Ebury Press, Random House, 2001.

Coates, Margrit. *Horses Talking.* London: Rider/Ebury Press, Random House, 2005.

Csikszentmihalyi, Mihaly. *Flow.* New York: Harper Perennial/Harper Collins Publishers, 1990.

Davies, John Anthony. *The Reins of Life.* London: J. A. Allen & Co., 1967.

Dedication to the National Park of Ainos. Cephalonia, GR: Museum of Natural History, Cephalonia and Ithaca, 1998.

Derek, Bo. *Riding Lessons.* New York: Regan Books/Harper Collins Publishers, 2002.

Diamond, Jared. *Guns, Germs, and Steel.* New York: W. W. Norton & Company, 1997.

Dorrance, Tom. *True Unity.* Bruneau, ID: Give-It-A-Go Enterprises/World Dancer Press, 1987.

Dromgoole, Glenn. *What Horses Teach Us.* Minocqua, WI: Willow Creek Press, 2002.

Engel, Cindy. *Wild Health.* New York: Houghton Mifflin Company, 2002.

Essays by Various Horsewomen. *Of Women and Horses.* Irvine, CA: Bow Tie Press/Fancy Publications, 2000.

Frowen, Deborah. *The Complete Guide to the Horse.* Hauppauge, NY: Barron's Educational Series, Inc., 1999.

Gladwell, Malcolm. *The Tipping Point.* New York: Little, Brown and Company, 2000.

Grandin, Temple, and Catherine Johnson. *Animals in Translation.* New York: A Harvest Book/Harcourt, Inc., 2005.

Gray, Peter. *The Organic Horse.* London: A David & Charles Book, 2002.

Gurney, Carol. *The Language of Animals.* New York: Bantam-Dell Publishing/Random House Inc., 2001.

Hillenbrand, Laura. *Seabiscuit.* New York: Random House, 2001.

Hintz, H. F. *Horses in the Movies.* New York: A. S. Barnes and Company, 1979.

Irwin, Chris, and Bob Weber. *Horses Don't Lie.* New York: Marlow & Company, 1998.

Kinkade, Amelia. *Straight from the Horse's Mouth.* New York: Thorsons/Harper Collins Publishing, 2001.

Kohanov, Linda. *The Tao of Equus.* Novato, CA: New World Library, 2001.

Mackay, Nicci. *Spoken in Whispers.* New York: Fireside, 1995.

Marks, Kelly. *Perfect Manners.* London: Ebury Press/Random House, 2002.

McCall, Elizabeth. *The Tao of Horses.* Avon, MA: Adams Media, 2004.

McCormick, Adele, Ph.D., and Marlena McCormick, Ph.D. *Horse Sense and the Human Heart.* Deerfield Beach, FL: Health Communications, Inc., 1997.

McGillivray, Debbie, and Eve Adamson. *The Complete Idiot's Guide to Pet Psychic Communication.* New York: Alpha/Penguin Group (USA) Inc., 2004.

Midkiff, Mary. *She Flies Without Wings.* New York: Dell Publishing/Random House, Inc., 2001.

Naparstek, Belleruth. *Your Sixth Sense.* San Francisco, CA: Harper San Francisco/ Harper Collins, 1997.

O'Conner, Sandra Day, and H. Alan Day. *Lazy B.* New York: Random House, 2002.

Olsen, Sandra. *Horses Through Time.* Boulder, CO: Roberts Rinehart Publishers/ Carnegie Museum of Natural History, 2000.

Pierson, Melissa. *Dark Horses & Black Beauties.* London: Granta Books, 2000.

Rashid, Mark. *Horses Never Lie.* Boulder, CO: Johnson Books, 2000.

Reeve, Christopher. *Still Me.* London: Arrow Books Limited, 1998.

Richards, Susan. *Chosen by a Horse.* New York: Harcourt Books, 2006.

Roberts, Monty. *The Man Who Listens to Horses.* New York: Random House, 1996.

Scully, Matthew. *Dominion.* New York: St. Martin's Griffin, 2002.

Sewell, Anna. *Black Beauty.* New York: Nelson Doubleday, Inc., 1877.

Sheldrake, Rupert, Ph.D. *The Presence of the Past.* Rochester, VT: Park Street Press, 1998, reissued, 1995.

Solisti–Mattelon, Kate. *Conversations with Horses.* Hillsboro, OR: Beyond Words Publishing, Inc., 2003.

Smith, Penelope. *Animal Talk.* Tulsa, OK, Council Oak Books, LLC, 2004.

Stone, Merlin. *When God was a Woman.* New York: Doubleday/Dell Publishing Group, Inc., 1976.

Storey's Horse-Lover's Encyclopedia. Pownal, VT: Storey Books: 2001.

Tellington-Jones, Linda, and Bobbie Lieberman. *The Ultimate Horse Behavior and Training Book.* North Pomfret, VT: Trafalgar Square Publishing, 2006.

The Language of Flowers. London: Frederick Warne and Co., 1868.

The spirit of RDA. London: Riding for the Disabled Association, 1995.

Timmons, Bonnie. *Hold Your Horses.* New York: Workman Publishing, 2003.

Williams, Marta. *Learning Their Language.* Novato, CA: New World Library, 2003.

Xenophon. *The Art of Horsemanship.* London: J. A. Allen & Company, 1962.

A Note to the Readers

I f you have an animal communication or healing story, which you would like to share, I would love to hear from you.

For more information, or to contact the author, go to:

www.HALevin.com

<http://www.HALevin.com>

Look for the next book in this series:

A History of Elephants Told by Elephants

Lookhang and Hal at the

Thai Elephant Conservation Center; Lampang, Thailand

About the Author

HOWARD ALAN "HAL" LEVIN was born in the Chinese Year of the Horse. He is an engaging speaker, who has a passion for writing inspiring books. Hal has enjoyed being an Outdoor Guide, Ski Patroller, Emergency Medical Technician, and Spiritual Healer. He has worked with many non-profit organizations, including volunteering at Humble Ranch (a therapeutic riding program for people with special needs). His home is in Steamboat Springs, Colorado.

Printed in the USA
CPSIA information can be obtained
at www.ICGtesting.com
JSHW012015140824
68134JS00025B/2432